Natalie Trice has had a successful, award-winning PR career spanning more than twenty-five years. She has worked with international TV channels such as CNN and Discovery Channel, fashion brands, large IT companies, entrepreneurs and start-ups. Today she's a senior PR director, as well as an ICF accredited coach, university lecturer and business mentor.

Cast Life: A Parent's Guide to DDH was Natalie's first book and sits alongside her charity, DDH UK, which supports thousands of people who deal with hip dysplasia, a condition one of her sons has been treated for over the past decade. Her second book, *PR School*, promises to take readers from zero to hero so they can do their own PR and feel as if they have their very own PR ninja sitting alongside them.

Natalie's a self-confessed relocation junkie, and while life in Leeds, Tokyo and London was fun, a life-changing move to south Devon in 2016 helped her find her place in the world.

When Natalie isn't at her desk, you'll find her surfing with her sons, walking on the beach with her dogs, or reading the papers in a shore-side coffee shop with her husband.

www.natalietrice.co.uk

How to Relocate

The Ultimate Guide to Starting Over
Successfully

by Natalie Trice

·····················

ROBINSON

ROBINSON

First published in Great Britain in 2022
by Robinson

10 9 8 7 6 5 4 3 2

A CIP catalogue record for this book
is available from the British Library.

ISBN: 978-1-47214-678-6

Typeset in Sentinel and Scala Sans
by Ian Hughes

Printed and bound in Great Britain
by Clays Ltd, Elcograf S.p.A.

Papers used by Robinson are from well-
managed forests and other responsible
sources.

MIX
Paper | Supporting
responsible forestry
FSC® C104740

Robinson
An imprint of
Little, Brown Book Group
Carmelite House
50 Victoria Embankment
London EC4Y 0DZ

An Hachette UK Company
www.hachette.co.uk

www.littlebrown.co.uk

How To Books are published by
Robinson, an imprint of Little, Brown
Book Group. We welcome proposals
from authors who have first-hand
experience of their subjects. Please set
out the aims of your book, its target
market and its suggested contents in an
email to howto@littlebrown.co.uk.

For Oliver, Eddie & Lucas,
my greatest loves,
my Devon darlings x

Contents

Introduction

My name is Natalie Trice and I'm a serial relocator.

If you're reading this book, I'm pretty sure you're in the throes of moving house, you can't stop looking at Rightmove or the prospect of relocating is something that's taking up precious headspace because you want to make that change but can't quite take the final, brave step to do so.

Whichever it is, hello, welcome, and get ready for the relocation read of your life.

Today I live in Devon, but my journey to finding the place where I truly belong took many twists and turns. It was a leap of faith, triggered by years of surgery for my younger son, that led us to living a happy life by the water. A life where I no longer feel like a square peg in a round hole, but instead like a mermaid who's found her tail and happily sits on the beach for hours, looking out across the water and knowing she is home.

I didn't always feel this at peace where I lived, which is why I've written this book, and I hope it will help you find true belonging, too.

When I was a child, I'd go to work with Dad in one of his haulage lorries as he moved people to start new lives, and, on the journey, I'd imagine the exciting adventures they were about to embark on as they started over somewhere new. At eighteen, I left the safety of a small town and headed 200 miles north to Leeds, which, on reflection, was a bigger culture shock than moving on to Tokyo where I taught English after graduating.

London was the next stop and, during my PR career, I moved from borough to borough, packing up my Ford Ka, getting to know the north, south, east and west of the city, with frequent trips across the world to progress my career.

When I had my first son, Eddie, I set up as a consultant, but things changed for ever when Lucas was born two years later, and was diagnosed with developmental dysplasia of the hip (DDH) at three months old. While Lucas now loves football, surfing and running on the beach with Eddie and our dogs, as a baby he endured endless operations; when he should have been learning to walk, riding a bike and jumping on bouncy castles, he was stuck in body casts and wheelchairs.

No longer going into London for work, I soon realised that living in the Buckinghamshire town where I'd grown up was suffocating me, and returning had been a mistake. Yes, it was pretty and house prices were rocketing; yes, the high street was paved with boutiques, high-end bars and restaurants; and yes, the magnificent bridge tourists flocked to visit was groaning under the weight of Lamborghinis and Range Rovers, but I was miserable. In the playgrounds and at the school gates there was a toxic undercurrent of competitiveness that ran deeper than the River Thames and I never felt like I fitted in – and, actually, I didn't want to.

I might have grown up there but after leaving at eighteen to go to university in Leeds, jumping on a jumbo jet to teach English in Japan, and then building a successful PR career in London, I really didn't feel that I was 'back home'.

As I navigated cliques and tried to block out the noise from the Joneses, I founded a charity, wrote my first book, did some freelance work and made memories with my boys. However, when we were told that Lucas needed to have his pelvis broken and remade – he was six at the time – something had to change. After a lot of soul-searching, I told my husband that either we went back to London or we moved to the sea, but I couldn't go on living somewhere that made me feel so unhappy. This might sound dramatic, but after years of trauma and heartbreak, combined with living somewhere I hated – somewhere I had to try to be someone I wasn't – enough was enough.

In the summer of 2016, and after I took the steps in this book, we packed up our suburban life. As I drove down the M5, a heavy weight of expectation and middle-class conformity left my shoulders. I rolled down the windows, put on my sunglasses and breathed for the first time in years. It felt so good, and I've never, ever looked back.

Believe me, this wasn't easy, and our move wasn't popular with everyone, but as I drive along the coastal road each morning to get the boys to school, I smile the biggest smile knowing that against all the odds, we did it.

Reaching our final destination (but probably not our forever home) was a dream that became a reality, and it's something I want to help you achieve too.

Moving won't change who you are, it won't fix your problems, and you can be sure that the removal men won't wave a magic wand as they close your new front door. However, when we leave the doubt behind, follow our hearts and lay down our roots somewhere we really want to be, wonderful transformations can happen.

I hope this book will help you find a new way of being and give you hope as well as a sense of freedom and direction so you can do what is right for you, and for those you love.

Did I stop and think, *Who am I to pack up my family to move to Devon?* Maybe a little bit.

Did I let the monkey on my shoulder hold us back from living our best lives? HELL NO!

Were there doubters who thought we were crazy to leave such a pretty town in the commuter belt? Yes, there were many, but that didn't matter, and their cutting comments made me even more determined to do it.

Were there days when I questioned whether we had done the right thing? No, not even when, three weeks after we moved, my six-year-old crashed into a table and cut his eye open. I had no idea where A&E was or how to get him there – rookie error – but a big ice cream on the beach that evening was all the evidence I needed to confirm we were home.

Do you see what I'm saying?

Fear can hold us back, and this is so true when it comes to making massive decisions, such as relocating.

Worrying about what others think can stop us from doing what our intuition is screaming out for us to do. What they believe to be right for us isn't what makes us happy, and it shouldn't impact our choices.

Now is the time to put a stop to the inner critic in your head that wants to keep you safe where you are, upsetting no one but yourself. If you feel that pull to move, now could be the time when you finally get out of your way, stop sabotaging your own success and happiness and start seeing how fabulous life can be when you're 'home'.

Our story is proof of what happens when you take that brave step, embrace your vulnerability and relocate to move your happiness forward.

I know not everyone's reason to move will be as dramatic as ours, and some people might have an even more urgent need to relocate, but I want you to know that I 'get it'.

I hope you can see that if I can pack up and successfully start again, so can you.

Don't think of this as just another book about moving, but the start of something new and exciting. Yes, relocating might scare you, but isn't being afraid for a little while worth it, if it means you end up somewhere so much better than where you're sitting right now?

There are always going to be reasons not to relocate. You don't have the time. You don't have the money. You don't know anyone where you want to move to. You can't afford the house of your dreams. You don't think your partner would want to move with you. You can't drive along country roads, and you certainly can't drive on the other side of the road. You don't speak French or Spanish or Chinese. Your dog doesn't like travelling in a car and your nan would never forgive you if you lived more than three miles away from her.

Stop!

These aren't valid reasons to stay somewhere that's not working for you, and I've got a feeling that, just by picking up this book, you know, deep down, that your heart belongs somewhere else. Somewhere on this planet that would make your heart sing, your pulse quicken when you look out of your bedroom window, and somewhere you would 100 per cent call 'home'.

You could be in Maidenhead, Morecambe or Montana –

wherever you are, ask yourself, 'Is this where I really want to be?' I'm guessing it's not quite right, otherwise why are you reading this?

While I'm confident that anyone moving house will find this book helpful, this is for people who want to make a big leap. Going from north to south, from one county to another, one country to another, or one continent to another.

Moving a couple of streets or going from the town you currently live in to one a couple of miles away can be tough, but it's not like packing up your life and starting all over again. Both scenarios are stressful in their own right, but relocating is a much bigger beast, and one that can throw up challenges and feelings you hadn't expected to encounter.

The reality of relocating is that it can impact more people than you think. As well as your partner, children and immediate family, there's your extended family, friends, neighbours, babysitter, the people you work with, the ones you play football with, and even the faces you wave at on the school run. With such a massive ripple effect of change come opinions from all corners on what you're doing, whether it's right (spoiler alert: only you know that), what could go wrong, why you should wait, and the effect your plans will have on them.

But if those people announced they were moving from Barnes to Brighton, would you voice your fears or concerns or put doubt in their heads? Hmmm, I'll leave you to ponder that thought.

As if relocating isn't tough enough, all of this extra noise can make it even harder to make that change, but that's why you're here and you can totally do it.

Through the pages of this book I have woven comments and quotes from friends around the world who have made a brave move – or more than one – as well as experts whose work I admire and whose advice I believe in. I hope their stories, examples and words of wisdom will answer your questions and ease your doubts, as well as inspiring you to make the decision that's right for you.

It is up to you what order you read the chapters in, but I do encourage you to add Post-it Notes to pages you want to go back to, scribble in the margins and underline the sections that resonate with you, so you can refer to them again during your journey. I also encourage you to have a relocation journal or notebook to hand so you can write down your ideas and thoughts as well as completing the exercises I have added to help you further create a vision and plan that will enable you to successfully do what you know is right for you.

So if you're currently thinking about relocating, you're in the process of doing so or you've taken bold steps towards change and are somewhere new, welcome, congratulations, and let's turn your dreams of successfully starting over into a reality.

Natalie

relocation, *n.*

/riːlə(ʊ)ˈkeɪʃən/

the action of moving to a new place and establishing
one's home or business there.

Chapter One

Is Relocating Right for You, Right Now?

'You're so lucky to live by the sea,' is something people say to me all the time, but as much as I love being here, it has absolutely nothing to do with luck, nothing at all.

What those friends see, as with so much of our digitally processed twenty-first-century lives, are the highlights, with a little bit of showing off. They scroll through my Instagram grid that is scattered with beach breakfasts, watch Facebook videos of us screaming as we surf in icy waters, and flick through the sublime sunsets across the horizon.

However, none of these seaside scenarios magically appeared overnight. Each single image is an insight into our relocation dream that took meticulous planning, a steely determination, and the steadfast belief that packing up and moving on was right for us.

If you have a fire in your soul that won't be quashed until you live somewhere that truly feels like home, I hear you.

Relocating isn't a guarantee of a 'happy ever after' and it won't make life perfect 24/7. What such a brave decision can do, though, is make earth-shattering differences to the way you live your life and how fulfilled you feel; and the sense of belonging it can bring is unreal.

It can open doors, change career pathways and allow you to make new friends. More than anything else, when it's done the right way, it can make you feel happier and more truly settled.

You can breathe fresh air, leave behind toxic workplaces and build something better than you ever imagined possible.

This isn't a pipe dream or something that's only for other people; this, my friend, is something for someone like you. What you do need, however, is to believe in yourself and to know, beyond doubt, that your decision is right for you. If you can do this, you're going to be one massive step closer to starting over successfully.

It's an Adventure

When you totally uproot your life and start over somewhere new, there's a layer of adventure and opportunity that gives you a feeling of excitement, but just as you think you've got this, worry and fear come into play and make you question your plans.

Your brain is wired to keep you safe, in your comfort zones and away from danger, but by doing so, it can keep you trapped, unfulfilled and unhappy.

Today, more than in any time in history, we are connected to the world around us and can seek out opportunities away from home. Long gone are the days of our grandparents and their grandparents, many of whom were born and bred in the same town, often living in the same house from birth to death, repeating the cycle and rarely questioning what else was out there to experience.

There's nothing wrong with this, and I'm sure it still makes some people happy, but there is a big, beautiful world out there. We can now live in far-flung places, in exciting cities and near movie-set beaches, rather than just visiting for a two-week holiday.

The purpose of this book is to give you the time and space, and maybe the permission you've been looking for, to dive deep into the idea of packing up. This isn't a decision to take lightly, and it's not something you can commit to having just read a single blog post or an inspirational story in a magazine.

You need the time to consider your next move, and this could take a week, a month, a year, or longer – it's a marathon and not a sprint, so don't feel pressured to set off today. If you go too fast, you may burn out halfway through and never get to the finish line. And that isn't what we're looking for.

There's no judgement on these pages, no raised eyebrows and no opinion. What I want is to ensure you're as informed as possible about your move, to see clearly why you're making dramatic changes, and the benefits that being bold and brave could bring to your life.

From my relocation experiences, those of my family, friends and the people I spoke to while writing this book, I can see that there's no right or wrong when it comes to changing where you live.

It isn't a one-size-fits-all experience that comes with a set of easy-to-follow checklists and a ready-made success plan, and that's not what this book is either. It can be a messy process that causes sleepless nights and arguments with loved ones, but life is short. Living in the place that's right for you is pretty fundamental for happiness, and if you aren't in that place right now, going somewhere that is isn't a crime; it's a necessity not to be overlooked.

Maybe you want to be closer to family so that your support network is enhanced, or perhaps you have care responsibilities for relatives. On the flip side, it could be that you want to be further away, and that is absolutely okay.

It could be the call of your career, or an opportunity to start over in a place you love without the pressure of a hefty mortgage to pay off.

For some it's the end of a relationship, whereas for others it's the beginning of a love affair they had given up on ever experiencing.

You might be following your children who have emigrated, or it could be that the time to downsize has arrived and that's taking you to pastures new.

Everyone has their reasons for staying or going, and I go into much more detail about all of this in the coming chapters of this book. However, whatever the reasons behind your move, and however excited you are about the potential changes on the cards, if it's going to be a success, you've got to be as prepared as possible.

What I'm clear about is that long-term changes don't tend to work out because of a knee-jerk reaction to life as it is now, and if you think that packing up and moving on will fix everything that's wrong immediately, it probably won't.

If we don't unpack some of our problems and learn to let them go, we can move to the most stunning tropical island in the world and still not feel settled, good enough, successful enough or rich enough.

Moving from one place to another isn't going to change who you are. You've got to do the inner work, as well as relocating, for all the pieces of the puzzle to come together.

Why Now?

Relocation is not a magic wand that will instantly transform your life and make you happy, so before we go any further, let's look at what's going on right now and whether moving is actually what you need.

Working through a simple but effective life audit can give you the space to look at where you are right now, what you want to change in your life, and how moving could make that happen. It can help cement your plans, as well as offering new perspectives and opportunities. Let's remember, no one is saying at this point that you can't change your mind, but what we're trying to do is look at the options available and what your next steps could be.

If relocation has been on your mind for a while, taking a life audit could help get your thoughts and feelings out of your head and on to a page, allowing you to look in black and white at what's really going on, what you're hiding from yourself and others, and what changes need to be made so you can lead a life you love, in a place that truly feels like home.

What's going well for you at the moment?

Think about what you're happy with right now. Maybe you love your job, your marriage is strong and you walk your dog with your best friend every day, and that makes your heart sing. We tend to go along on auto-pilot, but really thinking about those parts of your life you love, and that you'd have to give up if you moved away, can be strong enough to keep you where you are. Teens approaching GCSEs, a promotion at work or a group of besties you can't live without could stop your move now. Just think about what you'd have to give up to get the garden of your own that only moving would give you.

What isn't going so well?

This is a biggie and is often why people make a move. City crime, gang cultures, living close to your ex and their new partner, as well as dissatisfaction with work are all factors that can lead us to daydream about pastures new. Think about what these factors are for you and just how much of an impact they are having on your life and peace of mind.

What do you like about where you live now and what could be better?

Do you live close to some great cafés and bars? Is there a lake close by where you and your family go paddleboarding at the weekend? Are the schools really great? These plus points are enough to keep us where we are. However, maybe there aren't enough of the cultural experiences and diversity you value in the town you live in, or it could be the lack of green space nearby that worries you.

Being honest about what matters to you right now and assessing whether the good outweighs the bad can help you decide if a move is needed.

What would relocating change for you and for others in your life?

Looking at the bigger picture and what relocation could mean to others is hard, especially if it isn't going to be great for everyone. Being in Penzance might mean you can have a studio for your graphic design work, but if your partner needs to be in the city Monday to Friday, that could put pressure on your relationship and make you question the validity of your decision. It could be that your son and daughter both live near Manchester and, by moving to a village close by, you will see them more and be a bigger part of your grandchildren's lives than if you had retired and stayed in Surrey.

From losing friends or finding your tribe to quitting competitive school gates, having access to sports facilities or finally owning chickens, moving could bring many changes for you, so work out what they are, and whether they're enough to change the current status quo.

What impact would moving have on you financially?

It's really easy to make assumptions about how people are doing in life, but only you know the reality of your finances and it's always worth looking at the difference moving could make – both good and bad. It might be that the figures just don't stack up right now, and as frustrating as that can be, if you ignore the red flags, it could be really hard to start over successfully.

You might have to wait a few years, save up, get a second job and even downsize to move to your dream location, but if it's something you really want to do, you'll make it happen. Just don't give yourself a hard time, or a breakdown, trying to do it faster than your finances allow.

How do you feel about the community you live in?

This can be a really hard question to be honest about and uncomfortable to talk about with others who enjoy it. Maybe your town is safe, there's an ethnic mix and the community spirit is alive and kicking, but something is missing.

It could be that you're a single parent and don't feel a part of things in a village filled with the 2.4 family set-up, or you're part of the LGBTQ+ community and feel you simply can't be yourself.

Only you know how you feel, so think about it and see what comes up.

How would you be different if you were to move?

Relocating won't give you more confidence, it won't slow down the ageing process, and it's not a guaranteed step up the corporate ladder. Really thinking about what difference living somewhere else would mean can help you decide if this is right for you, and whether you can make a success of that change once the boxes are unpacked, your photos are on the walls and the fridge is fully stocked. Would you worry less about your children because they aren't getting the bus to school? If you moved to the countryside, would your anxiety be less intense because you could walk in the fresh air each day? There are so many things that could come into play here.

How would you be the same if you moved?

I've touched on this already, but whether you're in Bolton or Bath,

Hastings or Hamburg, Hampstead or The Hamptons, you're still going to be you. Moving isn't a quick fix to deal with the innermost emotions you feel, and it won't transform you from an introvert to a party animal, but your foundation could ease you into a better place.

List the qualities and emotions that make you you, and be honest; if you think relocating is going to change all of that, sit with it for a bit longer. Rather than a massive move, perhaps you need more holidays so you can recharge, therapy to deal with past trauma, or even a new job to boost your creativity?

Wherever I live, I'm still a coffee-drinking, magazine-reading, shoe-loving bookworm who values kindness, hates bad manners and never wants to be told what I can't do.

We can change our location, but we can't change who we are, so don't base a successful outcome on such a notion.

Do you have to move now, or can it wait?

You head over to Rightmove, spot the perfect house in your dream town and need to move NOW! Believe me, we have done this more than once and it's only as I head towards fifty that I've seen sense and not gone straight in with an offer on a property that would mean major structural works and eye-watering financial risks. I don't know your personal circumstances, but given the enormity of starting over, rushing in may not be the best tactic. If you can, take your time, read this book, do the exercises, let things settle, and get a plan in place.

If, for whatever reason, you need to move ASAP, I hope these pages will give you the guidance and support you need.

Are you worried about what people will think if you move?

While the majority of people will be pleased you're going somewhere that puts a skip in your step and a smile on your face, others will be sad you're leaving them and might feel like they are being pushed aside and rejected.

I talk about this more in Chapter Seven, but your job is to do what is best for you and not to make sure you're keeping everyone else happy. You can be sensitive to the feelings of others and consider their feedback, but if all that's stopping you from eating breakfast in the sun in Lanzarote is what Susan in HR might say, or how cross your cousins might be, I'd check in with yourself and ask what you really want in life.

What's the worst that could happen?

Loaded question, I know, but sometimes looking at the worst-case scenario can really put things in perspective. Really, the worst-case scenario is that things don't work out, and you need to have a rethink. Yes, that could be an expensive exercise, and you might have to eat humble pie, but isn't it better to have given it a go, to have left no stone unturned and explore your ideas? If we don't know, well, we don't know, so trying could be the best thing you decide to do.

What If You Don't Do It?

Let's stop for one moment here and think about what would happen if you didn't go. What would happen if you put this book down and carried on with the life you have at the moment? It's often this question that can make your decision for you.

Is it better to go for it – in a planned way, of course – and know that you did all you could to make your plans work, or to sit on the sidelines of your life making do?

Is what you have now enough, or, deep down, do you know you belong somewhere else and will never feel at ease where you are?

If that's the case, just think about what the emotional, mental and physical impact of not acting on your desires could be. Yes, it's scary, but aren't all the best things in life?

Relocation exercise

Let's get to work! Grab your relocation journal, a cuppa and write, doodle and scribble whatever comes to mind when you think about life right now.

What are you looking for from a big move? What impact would it have on you and those you love and care about? What excites and scares you about taking that big leap, and what goals would you smash by being brave and going for it?

This is also a time to think about how you'd feel if you stay where you are, and your dreams just stay dreams. What would you miss out on? What would you lose and how would it impact your life?

Where Do We Go Now?

I hope this first chapter has helped you gain clarity and if you're dedicated to this path, I can't wait to walk it with you.

Remember, even if you aren't ready to make the leap today, it doesn't have to be a 'no' for ever; it's just not right for you now. Things can change, so don't lose hope.

Packing up and starting over isn't easy, but sometimes being brave enough to take risks keeps the doubts at bay. Following our intuition can set us free and allow us to finally thrive, not just survive.

Chapter Two

The Reason Driving Your Relocation

Every person reading this book will be facing a unique set of circumstances when it comes to their relocation. My job is not to judge that choice, or to encourage you to go for it regardless, because I don't know you, and I can't give you a 'get out of jail free' card if things go wrong. What I can do is ensure you know why you want to make such a drastic move, because when this is crystal clear it makes everything else so much easier.

Having that deep-rooted reason won't ensure your chain doesn't fail on the day of completion, it won't stop resistance from others about your decision, and it doesn't mean money will magically arrive in your account to pay the stamp duty you hadn't factored in (see p.67), but when you do face challenges and things are feeling hard, you'll know why the hard work and heartache will be worth it.

If you think relocating is going to totally revolutionise your life, your mindset and your financial situation, I'm afraid it won't – or it won't for most people. However, if you know why you're making that decision, life could become easier; it might be possible to cut out the people who make things harder for you and it may offer new job opportunities. But you still need to do the work on the inside, because sustained internal change doesn't happen just by taking ownership of a new set of keys.

At twenty-two I took my heartache from Leeds to Tokyo and, guess what, when I arrived on the tarmac of Narita it was still there. It remained for months as I adjusted to a city that was as alien to me as not seeing my ex on a daily basis. The fast-paced way of life, teaching in Ginza and partying late into the night helped me move on, but it was time that healed me, not where I was – even though it proved to be a good distraction and allowed me to pay off my student debt.

If you don't feel content and satisfied in your life right now, relocating somewhere sunnier, bigger, smaller, trendier or cooler could simply act as a plaster to cover the bigger issues at play. Once the adrenalin and shininess of moving have died down, the same problems are more than likely to come up again and again, leaving you wondering what's going wrong.

If your restlessness is to do with your job, ask yourself if this would be solved by changing employers. If the answer is 'yes', then perhaps it's not a move that is needed but it could be a chat with your boss or some prospective job hunting.

If your friendship circle feels toxic, maybe you need a detox from that group rather than moving far away. If it's a break-up, you could find new, cooler places to hang out locally rather than upping sticks and heading to Oslo for some time out.

Feeling claustrophobic where you currently live? Having a spring clean and declutter could really change that space and is so much easier than a full-on relocation.

When you dig deep and look at what isn't working out, it might be that finding a new job, retraining, pivoting your career or finding new friends and hobbies could be all that is needed, so think really hard before you throw everything into packing boxes and start over. This is the time to take a look at each area of your life and to see what is making you happy and what you would like to change to feel even better.

Relocation exercise

To find out if it's a major geographical move you need, write down all the pros for moving, as well as the cons, and the things that are making you feel restless at the moment. These can be as big or small, significant or insignificant, as you like, but let the words and ideas flow thick and fast, and watch as the list builds.

There's no right or wrong, but quite often, taking words out of the filing cabinet of our minds and putting them down on paper can help us to think clearly about what we are doing and why. It could be that a few tweaks here and there are all you need to make changes.

If, having written down all your considerations, you still want to relocate, that's amazing and so exciting, but I'm glad you put in the work to make sure you came to the right conclusion for you.

If you're a little stuck on your reason for packing up, or can't quite put your finger on the feeling that is suggesting you need a change, I hope the following ideas will help you come to your own conclusion.

A Growing Brood

When we found out I was pregnant with our first son we were elated, but soon realised that our London flat wasn't going to fit our lifestyle any more. As our family grows, the space we need will increase, and while some people will remain in the vicinity but upgrade the square footage, others will take this as the opportunity to move somewhere else.

I know not every reader of this book will have children, and some of you may have grandchildren, but many will have to consider their dependents. Just as they change your life when they arrive, they continue to influence all aspects of your life, including moving.

Hannie Martin says, 'We moved from the border of Hertfordshire and Bedfordshire to lovely Devon because we were ready to start a family and wanted our children to have a more free-range childhood. I love that living here they get to grow up with access to the beach and moor, and have very much been allowed to be children.'

Abigail Marseilles adds, 'We moved from London to Devon when our daughter was one. She'd been poorly twice already with breathing issues, she was on medication, and we wanted cleaner air and less traffic.'

To Be Closer to Family

With divorce rates on the rise, longer life expectancy and a growing elderly population, people often relocate to be closer to family, and for a multitude of reasons. Whether it's following an acrimonious break-up and you need the support of family and friends to help with childcare, you want to be closer to your parents so you can take care of them as they age, or to have cousins and extended family members around as your children grow up, the reasons are varied but valid.

Becky Willoughby says, 'I moved 350 miles from Hastings to Kendal because, as a newly single parent, I needed the support of my parents.'

Rhiannon Spurgeon adds, 'I relocated to Devon because I knew I'd need my parents' help with my daughter.'

If this is the case for you, do talk to those you're moving closer to in order to scope out whether it's in line with their plans. We can quickly get carried away in our own little world, thinking others will be happy with our choices, but that can backfire – believe me. I'm sure you have their best interests at heart if they are struggling to maintain their garden and you're a pro with a mower, and the idea of having childcare on tap from your mum and dad could ease money issues, but don't assume this will fit with them. It might seem a strange thing to say, but while those closest to you might be sad if you're saying goodbye, piling on expectations and responsibilities to those who haven't seen a change coming could make your move less successful than you had imagined.

For Love

The things we do for love are crazy, romantic and sometimes downright foolish, and that can include following a beau somewhere new to be with them. When I met my husband I lived in London, while he lived out in the suburbs. In the end my commute was too much, and I moved out of the city and into a town for a while. It wasn't plain sailing, but we made it work in the end, and given that we are now in Devon, he did the same for me.

Jo Laybourn moved her life for love and says, 'I relocated my single life in Surrey for my now husband, who lived in Essex. We met in October, I put my house on the market the following Easter, moved in with him in the June, by which time we were engaged.'

Then there is Alison Schrecker, who adds, 'I relocated for love. I was living in Cambridge when I met Guy while skiing in Andorra during my first year of teaching; he was my ski guide. I moved into his house next to the Dome Roundabout in Watford five months later; the rest is history.'

Julie Naughton says, 'I met my husband in Blackpool where he was living at the time. We had a long-distance relationship for six months, then I moved from Newcastle to live with him. We used to look at the moon together out of the window from our separate houses whilst speaking on the phone. We are still together twenty-one years later.'

Leah Eser made a major move for love. She says, 'My first relocation was through my job, so in terms of logistics it was fairly straightforward, and my employer handled it all. Moving to America was slightly more complicated as I moved for love, so we had to get married before I could apply for my visa. I flew from Singapore to San Francisco, got married, then flew back to London where I applied and waited for my visa.'

To Get Away

Let's not wear rose-tinted glasses when we are looking at why we are relocating. Yes, for some it is to join the one they love, but some leave to escape something old and toxic, and to really start over.

May Coleman was raw and honest about her cross-country relocation, and says, 'I left a controlling relationship after a chance meeting rekindled an old love, leading me to suddenly relocate 150+ miles. I had a suitcase of clothes and a small amount of money in my purse. We didn't have a home, and I didn't have a job, car, bank account or passport. There were many hurdles to this situation, as solutions to each problem pretty much depended on the other being in place – you need ID to rent and get a job, but you also need an address to get ID!

'I was fortunate to have an amazing support network and slowly moved through the list, and six weeks later we had a home together, I had a car, and I started a new job. My bank account was finally open in time for my first payday. I have never been happier, and three years on I reflect on how I should have got myself a little more organised before I left, but sometimes the heart rules the head, and nothing is insurmountable when broken into smaller pieces.'

This type of relocation was also the reason for Jo, who says, 'I moved from Herts to Scotland as my abusive ex wanted to further his career and isolate me as much as possible from my family.'

Sue told me, 'I found my ex in bed with another woman. Fortunately I made the quickest relocation ever – I hired a car the same day ... moved the next day and as I had furnished his house, I left him with a cereal bowl and a spoon on an upturned cardboard box in front of his TV. I moved over 100 miles from Oxfordshire to a lovely house shared for two years and the rest is history! I'd probably shake his hand now for giving me this life!'

Every situation is going to be different, but if this is you, I send you love, and if you're in danger, please speak to someone you trust, or call the Refuge hotline for further support.

For Education

With education a major priority for parents, it's little wonder that relocating to get into the best schools, with outstanding Ofsted reports and filters into decent senior offerings, is commonplace. While my husband and I did this, it didn't work, and I would 110 per cent recommend not moving in the summer holidays, only to look at the school everyone raves about to realise it isn't for you – true story. But we live and learn and now you don't need to make the same mistakes as me.

It was a different outcome for Melissa Richards, who told me, 'We relocated from London to Tunbridge Wells via Basel. Having had my twins, I was off work and my husband was working for a client in Basel. To save him being away Monday to Thursday, we suggested that we move out there for the duration of the project. At the end of the project we knew we didn't want to go back to London, because we wanted to be somewhere "safer" for the kids and with good school prospects. We chose to be in Tunbridge Wells for their good primaries that feed into local grammar schools. The kids start in September (having worked hard to pass the Kent test to qualify to enter), so it worked out for us.'

You might love where you live now, but if there's a lack of choice when it comes to schools, a selective system you don't agree with or a change in headteacher means where you were going to send your kids now makes it less appealing, relocating is an option, and could be less expensive than choosing the independent route if you plug to stay where you are.

Amanda Egleton adds, 'We moved from Uxbridge, Middlesex, to Buckinghamshire thirteen years ago for schools. It was the best decision we made, and we feel very lucky to live where we do now.'

More Space

I'm not just talking about the number of bedrooms or whether there's an attic that can be converted into a home office, but also the space around you and the environment you spend your time in. Living in Tokyo was pretty intense but at twenty-two I could cope with being pushed on to a packed commuter train and people being insanely close to me on the street; doing the same with a baby and toddler in tow ... maybe not so much.

Relocating gives you the chance to reassess your location in terms of how built-up the place you live in is, how close the open spaces and parks are, how easy it is to get out into nature and build a life beyond concrete jungles, malls and motorways.

Anne made this kind of move, and says, 'We wanted space of our own and house prices in Surrey were not helping. I wanted to be more rural, and we found the perfect place, close enough to town but right on the edge of the countryside in a little friendly village.'

This was the case for Louise Pallister Turley, who said, 'It was simple for me, as it was all about the sea! We were in Bristol, but I wanted a balanced life by the sea for kids to grow up in, and it worked so well.'

Space could also be about finally having a garden, rather than just window boxes, so you can grow the plants and herbs that will make your life feel like yours.

The Weather

Do you ever stop and think, *Is there more to life than where I am right now?* I'm writing this book in the summer of 2021 and it's extremely warm, and while the sunshine beats on my back as I swim in the sea, it's just too hot for me. This is further proof that Devon is a way more appropriate place for me to live than, say, New Zealand, but each to their own and it could be that is exactly where you want to move to for precisely that reason.

Emma Maslin was a weather mover. She says, 'I moved to Australia for the sunshine, originally on a two-year work secondment. I met my husband there. Married there. Came home seven years later to be close to family when we'd had our first child.'

Closer to home, Jane Hanford adds, 'I couldn't bear the grimness of commuting and working in the city any more. One dark, rainy January evening, having gone from the tube to the train to the bus to get home, I hit a wall. It was like my soul was dying inside me. I thought, *I can't do this any more.* Twenty months later I was living in beautiful Lyme Regis, and, honestly, I am so happy. I have never looked back.'

To Experience the World

While we can visit other countries and find out more about them courtesy of the internet, social media and television, there's something real and special about living in the places that inspire us, and this can be a very real reason to relocate.

Jessica Silva says, 'I wanted a different pace of life and to experience living in a different country. I wanted to learn to speak another language well, and for my son to have the chance to be bilingual. So, we moved from London to Mallorca. Haven't regretted it for one day. The light, the access to the sea, and the colours in the countryside make me smile every day.'

For Helen Moore it was a similar reason for her relocation, 'We went from London to the countryside north of Limoges, France. Our boys were five and three, and the schools were shocking in our bit of London, as there were not enough places, and we thought that it would be a gift to the kids to be properly bilingual and European. We were both able to work remotely as long as we had internet and access to an airport or train station, and it also allowed us to dump the big mortgage. Love it – never regret it for a second.'

Rachel Barker was young, child-free and simply thought, *Why not?* She adds, 'Everything looked so bright, clear and sparkly over in Australia. Our life at the time in the Midlands couldn't really compete. Looking back, it was a bigger move than we probably gave ourselves credit for, I was twenty-three.'

You're Part of the Forces

At several of the schools my sons have attended, their friends have come and gone, but none more so than those whose parents have been in the forces.

Nicole Llewellyn knows about this well and says, 'I relocated several times with my husband as he was in the forces, and it was the same when I was a child as my dad was in the forces. I returned to my place of birth both times, to be near family, close to the sea, and because Wales is in my blood.'

Sarah Bramall was an army wife and says, 'We had lots of relocations. We went from Leeds to Plymouth to Reggio Calabria to Harrogate to Thirsk to Surrey to Harpenden, and, on top of this, my husband was deployed to Bosnia and Iraq in that time – bonkers! The hardest was when I was twenty weeks' pregnant with our first; the best was moving from Plymouth to Reggio Calabria in the far south of Italy.'

While I love to move, I am in awe of the frequency and speed with which many military families move and, while I know it's a part of the job and it comes with the territory, I am pretty sure it can't be easy to constantly be relocating. If this is you, I hope there is support in place to help you adjust with each move.

A Move Driven by Work

Work is a reason why many people relocate: a promotion that's just too good to turn down, the HQ of a company moving or the chance to be part of something new and exciting, maybe with a hotel chain, tech company or even starting up on your own.

Denise Spragg says, 'I moved to Somerset from just outside Bedford to set up our brand-new, from-scratch and non-franchise business with my husband, 180 degrees in the opposite direction from our previous jobs, leaving the place where I'd always lived, our friends and family – and I wouldn't change a thing. We'd been looking for about a year, considering all areas of the UK, and visited lots of places in the south-west to catch the vibe of the place – much time spent people-watching in coffee shops! We settled on Taunton, found our beautiful business premises, and then had to find somewhere to live.'

In 2010 Lucy Davies relocated from London to Cheshire, and says, 'I decided to relocate because I was burned out from a stressful corporate career in Canary Wharf, London. I was leaving a toxic job and wanted to find a more joyful life. Having lived in London for a decade, I was ready for a change – and my parents were retiring back to the north-west, where they both grew up. It seemed like the natural choice to head here too!'

Debbie Favell adds, 'My husband was approached by a recruiter for a Canadian company who were interested in him working for them. They arranged for us, as a family, to visit for a week and to see the two different cities that the company was offering relocation to. It was a crazy, fun and tiring seven days, with five flights (two transatlantic and three internal), three cities, three time zones and three children aged seven, five and one. After returning home and lots of discussions and research, we decided to take the plunge. The company lawyers took care of the immigration paperwork whilst we had to sell our home, arrange shipping of our belongings, find somewhere to have as a base for six weeks when we arrived, sell our cars, decide what belongings we would take and what we needed to get rid of, prepare the children for the move, sort out finances, arrange for supplies of prescribed medications to take, say goodbye to friends and deal with a sudden family bereavement.'

This kind of relocation might seem easier on paper, but it still comes with its own set of concerns and issues, and if you don't really want to go, or you're going because it's for a family member or your partner, it could cause friction and resentment. I had totally forgotten about this, but when I first met my now husband, I was offered a relocation package to Washington as I was working for Discovery Channel, and they had a post that would've been perfect. The timing wasn't right, but wow, it could've been amazing and maybe he could have come with me, but we didn't think that eighteen years ago and now will never know.

Downsizing

While I'm anticipating many readers of this book will be looking to move to a bigger space when they relocate, for some this will be an exercise in downsizing, something that can be an emotional experience. You may well have spent your life trying to create more space, and then lived in your home for many years, with the fabric of the four walls currently surrounding you full of memories that you might not want to walk away from.

Downsizing can be difficult if it wasn't part of the plan – an acrimonious divorce, your children moving out of the family home, or the death of a partner – but it happens, and you can get through this.

It could be that staying in the village you currently live in is too painful after a separation, or you might want to finally live by a lake, or closer to your children, which means that downsizing is necessary. What I would say is that downsizing isn't a weakness or a sign that life is coming to an end. Instead it is the next chapter in your life and one you can embrace and find positives in too. Alison Chown says, 'My mum downsized and chose the house she's in because she loved the garden!'

If you aren't 100 per cent sure that it's time to downsize and relocate, signs you might want to look for include: rooms you no longer use; your garden becoming too much for you to look after, even though you have spent decades making it beautiful; a feeling that you're too far from the children and grandchildren you want to share your life with; the bills getting bigger and bigger; you're ready to stop driving but transport links aren't great where you live right now.

Whether you're excited to relocate as you downsize, or are coming at it with doubt and trepidation, if you can look at this as a new chapter, and follow my steps to finding somewhere next, I hope you will be happy somewhere new.

Retirement Beckons

There's no set age range for the reader of this book, so I imagine some of you will be retiring and looking at moving in your later years. Now I don't know you at all, but I would say, take your time before you make another big move, because giving up work alone is a massive life change.

If you've spent decades living in a city, surrounded by coffee shops and restaurants and with easy access to entertainment and public transport, rural life with one bus a week and a single post office may make you feel cut off, especially when the days get shorter and you're home alone.

You might be considering a relocation so that you're closer to your family. With more time on your hands you could be able to see them more often, maybe help with the grandchildren on a regular basis and strengthen familial bonds. This will be easier without the ties of work holding you back and restricting your time.

It could be that a career in the City meant you haven't had the time to take care of a garden, but see this as a chance for you to pick up a pitchfork and start planting the vegetables and herbs you always meant to grow. You might long to be able to swim in the sea or go walking on the hills at the weekend, things that were the reserve of holidays when you were working full time and bringing up your family.

There are so many things to consider when you retire and it's a massive time of change and adjustment for many people, so make sure you're ready to change every aspect of your life in one go, or does this need to be a phased transition so you don't make a rash decision that leaves you feeling bored and out of place?

To Be Closer to Nature

Let's not forget that being closer to nature is another reason people relocate. Concrete cities and snazzy suburbs are all well and good, but if getting out into the countryside, cycling in the hills or sailing are things you want to do more often than when you're on holiday, it could be an indication that it's time to make a move.

Looking out over Canary Wharf is stunning at sunrise, but so is being on a paddleboard in Lyme Regis. Yes, this is a big change, and there are many other factors at play when it comes to city vs. countryside, town vs. seaside, but it's something that might be a factor in your desire to relocate and if so, good for you.

There will be reasons I haven't covered in this list of relocation triggers, but I hope I've included the vast majority of them and that there is something here that resonates with you so you can move forward with your plans.

While other people might offer their advice and thoughts, these factors can only be decided by you. You're the one who has to live with the results, so try to listen to your thoughts and follow your intuition, so you can make a choice that will allow you to successfully pack up and start again, and not only survive, but thrive.

Relocation exercise

In your relocation journal, write a list of things you like about where you live at the moment, what your home offers you, how you feel about the community, leisure facilities, the friends you have and the family around you. Then consider what somewhere new would need to offer you to make the move a success. Do you need a flat rather than a house? Is it important to have a bedroom for your grandchildren? Are you still driving or is public transport going to be a key consideration? There's so much to think about here, I know, but this is the time to put your cards on the table, dream big and have fun plotting your future.

Chapter Three

Set Your Destination

With your reason for relocating settled in your head and written down on paper, you can zone in on where you want to be.

If you're reading this and already know where you're going, great, but even if that's the case, I'd encourage you to keep reading this chapter to double and triple check that you're truly happy with your choice and haven't left any stone unturned.

If you're in the process of making that all-important location decision, I'm so excited for you, because the world is your oyster. This is the time to search for your happy place, and if you flit from one idea to another right now that's fine. Considering the total surface area of Earth is about 197 million square miles, there's a world of possibilities out there for you to explore and places to make home.

Getting clear on where you want to be is really important if you want to successfully start over – sorry for stating the obvious, but you only need to watch property programmes on TV to see the impact getting it wrong can have. Whether you're reading this because your teenagers are approaching university, you're looking for a fresh start after a divorce, your partner has a life-changing work decision to make or it's time to retire, you need to take your time and find the ideal location for you.

When I moved 200 miles to go to uni in Leeds I looked at the glossy photos in the prospectus, and based my choice on those. Teaching in Tokyo at age twenty-two wasn't so much a considered choice as travelling to ease a broken heart, and when I landed back in London, I moved in with a friend because she needed a flatmate, not because I fell in love with the Caledonian Road. Devon was a more considered choice and one that took around a year from conception to champagne. This might not seem long, given that in that time I also wrote a book, launched a charity and my son had yet another orthopaedic operation, but on my relocation CV, that was quite a lot of time, and it has been my most successful move.

As well as knowing your reasons for moving, you'll also have your own timeframe. A major move with work might see you going from Manchester to Hong Kong in a couple of months because that's what the team needs, but settling in the Welsh mountains, your lifetime dream, could take years. Getting the location for your move right is key to a successful relocation, so go at your own pace. Let's look at the options.

Village, Town, City or Something Else?

Like many of my friends, in my teens and twenties I lived in cities, had crazy adventures, went to tropical islands, lived in shared flats and had fun. When I had my children I wanted to be part of the community, where it was quieter, where I could be more connected to my surroundings. I'll admit, as much as I'd hoped that would be in the town where I grew up, that wasn't the case. In the end, it was being somewhere new, having the chance to start over on a blank canvas and create the life I wanted, by the sea, that made home home for me.

As you read these pages, consider whether where you want to move to is going to make your heart sing.

Do you want to move to a city, town, village or a hamlet? Maybe the dream is somewhere free from neighbours altogether, with only the birds and Mother Nature for company? Note of warning with that one: the toddlers you're moving with now will become teenagers who will need a taxi (aka you) to take them places for years to come if there isn't a local bus or train service for miles. Forward planning should come into the mix.

Are you looking for an eclectic mix of cultures and generations in a city where you can enjoy the buzz of galleries and bars and grab a skinny flat white on every other corner? Or do you want to get out in the fresh air, embrace wild swimming and make tea from the mint you're growing in your back garden?

Do you need good schools and efficient traffic links, or are pristine golf courses, quiet country lanes and rambling on your radar for this relocation?

For some people, being in a tight-knit community close to your extended family and the friends you grew up with is going to be top of your priority list. However, if, like me, you enjoy a little more anonymity and autonomy, that could be suffocating and leave you feeling trapped and frustrated.

Relocation exercise

In your relocation journal, spend some time brainstorming the villages, towns, counties and countries you want to move to. Dream big, write lists, draw maps, add images and start to piece together what home looks like for you.

Weather and Climate

Something many people commented on when we announced our move to Devon was that it rains here all of the time, and what would we do with all that wet weather? At the time it annoyed me, I felt they were trying to put us off leaving, and while they had a point (don't tell them), I wasn't going to let it dampen my spirits. Yes, it rains, but not every day. Plus, I love walking on the beach in the rain because it's a time when it's quiet. I've swum in an outdoor pool in the rain in December, which left me feeling exhilarated for days, and there's something magical about surfing as the rain falls around you and the waves take your body back to shore.

For me, the freedom of being here and living a life I love far outweighs the weather. It's actually warmer here than anywhere I've lived in the UK, and lighter, which makes those dark winter afternoons more bearable and gives me longer to take the dogs out while it's light. But this wouldn't be for everyone, so when you're making the decision to relocate, you need to look at these factors.

Debbie Favell was honest with me and admitted that Canadian weather was quite a change from England, and says, 'Prairie winters were an eye-opening (or shutting) experience. Regularly in the -20s (°C), sometimes lower, and, due to open, flat land, wind-chill factors can make it feel like -40°C. It literally freezes any moisture inside your nose and your eyelashes. You learn to layer clothes, have remote start on your car, and, complete mind-boggler, plug your car in at night so it doesn't freeze. We adapted really quickly to the weather, bought good snow boots, coats, hats and snow tyres for the car.'

You might think that wall-to-wall sunshine is amazing, but Louise Goss was surprised by her reaction to this: 'Moving to Australia, I found the heat of mid-summer quite stifling at times. When you're not on holiday, you can't swim in the sea every day! Raising babies in the summer was the hardest thing as you couldn't dress them in anything, but had to keep them covered to protect from the sun! I missed the distinct change in seasons you get here, although you do get it further south.'

For Jo March it was a similar story, and she adds, 'Thailand has three seasons – hot; hot and wet; and very, very hot. Stepping outside in Bangkok during the hot season is like stepping into a filthy hot sauna. When I worked I wore more make-up than ever before (or since), as I was constantly red-faced, hot and bothered. When I stopped working, I mostly gave up on make-up as it just melted. I learnt to drink *lots* of water and stay properly hydrated the hard way. I got a UTI which morphed into a nasty kidney infection – I had a couple of hospital stays as a result as I was so poorly. My wardrobe was full of natural fibres – mostly cotton and linen plus some silk – as anything artificial was too hot, and I never fully adapted.'

With all of this said, if you have a say in where you're going to live (I'm guessing the RAF don't give a pick-and-mix on base destinations), you need to think about the weather, a bit like me at twenty-two with my sensitive skin being welcomed by Narita airport, in July, with 90 degrees and 99 per cent humidity, a rookie error and one I know you won't make.

Relocation exercise

In your relocation journal answer the following questions and start to link the weather to the locations you're considering moving to:

- Are you a hot or cold person?
- Do you love the sun?
- Do you like walking to work in icy conditions (watch those hips)?
- How do your kids feel about living in snow for many months of the year?
- How much rain can you live with?
- How much dry weather can your plants survive in?
- Do you like lighter days to ease mental health issues?
- If you're a big runner, would the dark nights and cold days in Scotland be good for you?

Lifestyle Factors

I looked at many forums and read endless articles while researching and writing this book, and the lifestyle factors people list as non-negotiables were as varied as the way they take their tea. No two people had identical relocation criteria, so what you're looking for will be different to anyone else, and may be in conflict with those you're moving with, which can be tricky.

Being clear on what's important isn't selfish, it's sensible, because, if those early-morning spin classes followed by a green smoothie in a trendy bar set you up for a productive day at work, and you can't find them when you move, your job performance will suffer, your fitness will take a hit, and you'll be unhappy, so that successful result won't happen.

If being outside and getting muddy on mountain bikes is your thing, living in central London probably isn't going to be right for you. However, if you're a drama lover and want a job in the arts, being in the heart of Soho and theatreland may well bring you to life and help light you up.

Having a thing for shopping and eating out at the weekends means a hamlet in rural Wales may not be the right lifestyle location for you, but I know that Cardiff has some awesome malls and excellent cafés and that could tick more boxes for a successful move.

It's at this point you need to dig deep and really think about the activities you love doing now, and want to be able to do if you move somewhere new. You might think that a farmhouse restoration project on the moors would be amazing and fulfil your desire to grace the pages of *Country Living* one day, but if you rely on decent broadband for work, funding this dream right now might not be possible.

Think about what is important to you – and to those you're moving with – and what you can't live without, because if you move and you don't have those things, I'm pretty confident you won't be happy.

Relocation exercise

In your relocation journal, start making a list of all the lifestyle factors that are important for you. This is something you'll probably want to come back and add to, so keep a few pages clear for this work.

Do You Need to Commute?

While COVID changed the way people work for ever, not everyone has the luxury of working close to, or at, their new home. For the first year we were in Devon, my husband went back to London on a regular basis, so we needed to be close to the motorway and a decent train service, making rural north Devon a no-go.

You might think going back and forth from the new place to the old isn't a big deal, but give it a while, add traffic jams, late trains, having to stand in the cold and dark, and you might rethink this.

Tim Griffiths also moved to Devon and says, 'Take your time to research the local area and where you would like to live, as some areas can be quite remote. We had to be near the M5 for my job as I needed to get back to London every month, so needed to be close to the A303 and M3. In the end we found a house we love that is near a local train station which goes all the way to London Clapham and Waterloo without having to change, and the airport in Exeter is just down the road, which we have used a great deal.'

Factor commuting into your plans, and check websites like Rightmove as they include details about the proximity to transport hubs. Just knowing how accessible the location is can really impact your choices. On paper it might look like getting from Pangbourne into London is easy, but add getting to the station, finding a parking space, the time on the train, as well as the tube or walk at the other end, and it could become less appealing. This is the time to do that research and get it right, so look at the options and get a feel for what's realistic and sustainable for you.

What About the Children?

As I write this book, I'm thinking ahead to my son learning to drive. Our village is rural but there is a busy main road that connects us to the outside world, and one that is becoming increasingly dangerous and turning into an accident hotspot. Six years ago, this wasn't on my radar as the boys were playing with cars, not driving them. As time goes by, your requirements change, and while we cannot protect our loved ones from the world, nor can we see into the future and make our plans failsafe, some future pacing, when it comes to moving with kids, is a good idea.

It might feel like moving out of Nottingham and relocating to a Suffolk village is perfect when you have tiny tots who love the park and jumping in muddy puddles, but fast-forward ten years and that one bus a week and no senior school for twenty miles may not serve you so well. Equally, if your tweens are used to a tiny school in the middle of nowhere, but your relocation involves a transatlantic flight and taking the New York subway to school, that could feel pretty intense and end in tears (although thinking about it, that could be very cool).

Relocation exercise

There isn't a perfect, forever solution when it comes to relocating with kids, and one day they'll leave too, but I'd suggest drawing up your list of ideal locations and then plotting the pros and cons for family life in each. From schools and playgrounds to youth clubs, decent street lighting and public transport, take all these elements into consideration. Oh, check in with your kids and see what they want – age permitting, obviously.

I talk more about relocating with kids in Chapter Eight so skip ahead if this has piqued your interest.

Safety

Crime rates and feeling safe are something I really thought about before we came to Devon. With two sons, who I'm sure will want to embrace their teenage years by going out with their friends and venturing further than our village, we wanted to live somewhere that was relatively safe. I can't control what they do for ever, but I wanted to eke out their childhoods for a little longer, and while it would be naive of me to think that there are no dangers where we live, I feel they're safe here.

The reality is anything can happen, but once you have a shortlist of places you're considering moving to, a quick online search can help you get a feel for crime rates, as well as safety. It's more likely that a big city will have higher crime rates than a sleepy village, but don't let this put you off, and it's also about how you feel somewhere. I'm happier walking around central London at 11 p.m. than Newton Abbot; the stats might say the big smoke is more dangerous, but personally, I feel safer there.

Lauren Malone, business coach and mindset expert, is a great example of moving due to safety concerns, and she says, 'Growing up in the countryside I knew I didn't want to live in the city for ever. I loved Bristol but wanted fresh air and space when I decided to start a family, and my husband, who was born and bred in Bristol, agreed. I bought a lovely little two-bed terrace in Bristol in 2012. I'd heard the area was "up and coming", I had friends who lived there and at the time there was zero stamp duty. Luke and I were married in May 2018 and knew that we would probably start looking into starting a family and move out of Bristol in 2019. In July 2018 we were burgled. We had both left the house at the same time that morning and a few minutes later someone broke in. They didn't take much but they made a right mess, and it was how this felt that spurred us on to make changes. We felt like the house wasn't home any more. It had been invaded and contaminated. We didn't feel unsafe, but we did feel the security and sanctuary had gone. It was then we started talking in earnest about moving and took full advantage of apps like Rightmove and Zoopla. We initially were looking at an area just up the M5 (the direction towards my parents). On these apps you put in the mile radius and as we were so flexible and just exploring ideas I put in 10 miles. That brought up an area called Lydney that I'd never heard of. Actually, Lydney is much further than 10 miles driving from where we were looking because there's a huge river in the way, but I'm so glad it came up because we decided to check it out. The house prices were reasonable, so it definitely seemed worth it. We fell in love with the Forest of Dean on our first visit and knew it was the area to focus on. At the time we also thought we would be commuting to work in Bristol so that was a consideration. In November we found our house in a beautiful, quiet little village. I remember asking Luke if he was really up for it when we went to put in an offer. Having grown up in a small village I knew what to expect but was worried he didn't know what he was letting himself in for ... no twenty-four-hour shop on the doorstep! We accepted an offer on the house in Bristol within two weeks of putting it on the market and our offer had been accepted. The house prices in Bristol had shot up so we were delighted to not only be up-sizing, but we also had some extra money! We had decided that commuting wasn't really what we wanted and actually with the extra money we had made from the house sale, we could set up our own businesses.'

The question of safety may be just one of the many pieces of your relocation puzzle, but I feel that it's my duty to cover this element, and even if you look at the local police website, newspapers and online groups, it's a start.

Ethnicity and Sexuality

It pains me that in this day and age, I still see people looking for advice in Facebook groups and online forums for recommendations of places that are accepting of all ethnicities and sexualities, but it's something that comes up time and time again. You need to feel comfortable where you live, so do your research, visit where you want to live and work out if it's going to be right for you.

We want to live in a world of acceptance and tolerance, but we know that sadly isn't always the reality, so start asking family friends, as well as your wider network, about places you're thinking about moving to. Search out information online and be clear on what you need from a community.

Religion

For some people, living in a community that supports their spiritual needs is not only important, it's vital to finding the right place to relocate to and live in. You might be moving to be closer to a certain church group or to make it easier to visit a synagogue now you aren't driving. If your faith is very much a part of your life, and you're looking for support from people who share your religion, make this part of your search, and I'm sure your current support network will be able to offer you connections with people and guidance.

Kathrine McAleese gave me a real insight into this. She says, 'A decent church sees a new person and wants them to feel at home, so they'll say hello, help them find their way about. That instantly gives you someone you "know" next time you go. If they're really good and they have coffee after the service, you'll likely get introduced to a few more people. When I moved to Norfolk, that's exactly how I met the woman who would become my bestie there – someone spoke to me when I came in on my own, and then having pointed out coffee and cake after the service she introduced me to Alaina who had a fabulous manicure in my favourite colour ... so that hooked me up to a nail salon and someone I had something in common with. BOOM.'

It's All About the Broadband

It's all very well to say you're going to move and work from home, but if you rely on the internet, you need a decent connection, and speaking from experience this isn't always as easy as it might seem. Even if you love that six-bedroom house in Cornwall, with the thatched roof and the lake in the garden (and all for less than the cost of a studio flat in Notting Hill), if you can't load up Google, order paper on Amazon or call your boss, it's not going to work. It could make your relocation unsuccessful because you'll be frustrated, uncontactable and, potentially, unemployable.

Now, if you're moving to be off grid, and being connected to the outside world 24/7 isn't a key factor for you, go ahead and buy that dream boat house, but if you aren't ready for a less techy existence, still want to order from Asos, and want to be able to like your mum's posts on Facebook, consider the internet connection.

Liz Graveny's move to Devon was a success, but the tech side of it, not so much. 'In the first week of our move, when I couldn't get any business broadband or a mobile signal due to our house being at the end of a cul-de-sac, I wondered if we had done the right thing. The mobile signal continues to be very sporadic even now and our London friends and family are flabbergasted when they visit!'

Clare Mackenney says, 'We have a Facebook group for our Devon village, and I've seen people online say, "We've moved here and our broadband or Wi-Fi is terrible. Can anyone recommend a good provider?" And the answer is NO! We don't have fibre so no matter who you go with it will always be bad. People from towns assume that it will be good everywhere. So I would advise people to really do their research on local message boards for the real answer, not what BT or the estate agent tells you.'

And that told you!

Finally, Phil Leivesley, Senior Mortgage Adviser at award-winning mortgage broker MB Associates, says, 'If you're not sure where to move to, the consumer website *Which* has advice on finding the right location for you. It offers an area comparison tool that will give you a chance to see how your chosen area compares to the national average. It contains information on schools, average house prices and happiness scores.'

Relocation exercise

Create a relocation vision board that covers all of the elements we have looked at in this chapter so you can start to get a clear picture of where you want to be. Put it up in your kitchen so you can see it each day, add things when you see them and when you finally make your relocation a reality, why not frame this and put it in your new home as a reminder that you successfully started over?

Chapter Four

Visit, Visit and Visit Again

When you've decided where you want to move to, visit, visit and visit again. Then, if you can, go again!

It's one thing to think you want to live by the sea, but August, when the sun is shining and the deckchairs are brightening up the beach, presents a very different place to the cold, foggy conditions come mid-January, when everyone is back at home and things are bleak. I personally love it when the holidaymakers go home, the car parks are empty and I can get a coffee without queuing for an hour, but this doesn't work for everyone, and I know people who've made the move and not warmed to the ebb and flow of seasonal changes.

I know not all timeframes or -zones allow for this, but visit in the rain, in the sun (it may well be too hot), in the summer, in the winter, go morning, noon and night, and then do it again, and if you do, you'll be glad you did because it could save a move that isn't right for you.

Going to visit pastures new as often as you can before making your move is something Charlie Lemmer, aka The Healthy Home Therapist, a buying agent and serial relocator, agrees. She told me, 'I would advise you to get to know an area as well as possible before you move. Rightmove and other search engines are excellent tools, but unless you walk the streets of an area, you don't know whether that gorgeous townhouse is right next to a train line, whether the number 4 bus stops directly outside your door and will keep you awake for the next five years. It's difficult to get everything right unless you're an expert, but I generally spend at least two weekends in an area so I get the feel for where I want to be and will consider transport links, amenities, schools, etc. This makes your search so much easier online, otherwise it's a bit like looking for a needle in a haystack.'

Halfway to Leeds, at the start of my uni adventures, I asked my mum if we were there yet. Er, no! I'd been given a conditional offer, got my grades, packed my posters and DMs, but had no real idea where I was going. Admittedly I was eighteen, there was no internet, and Google Maps was not a thing, so when I arrived in the north of England, after a childhood in the Home Counties, to say I was out of my depth was an understatement. Call it innocence or naivety, but I hadn't done any real research into where I was going to be living for the next four years. I took the plunge, lucked out with my roommate in my first year and made Leeds my home. It's a place I'm still very fond of, but may not have ended up my home at all had I visited in the first place.

Would I suggest you pack your bags, get in your car and hope for the best? No! While a relocation to a new country may be prohibitive when it comes to endless visits, my advice to you is to visit as many times as you can.

Lucy Davies, says, 'My practical advice for someone looking to relocate is to spend as much time as possible in your new location before you actually move. Take time to really get to know it – and definitely think about how to start a social life if you don't have connections there already.'

Debbie Favell thinks the same: 'My advice to you is to research, research, research! Google, Facebook groups, visiting – if possible – and finding local knowledge from people will be invaluable in deciding on a relocation.'

Before we moved to Devon we visited a lot; not excessive amounts, but enough to know where we wanted to be, and, just as importantly, where we didn't want to be! Yes, it meant many trips down the M5, with grumpy kids in the back of the car on a Friday night in backlogged Bristol traffic, as well as hotel bills and lots of takeaway coffee, but it was worth it when we realised we had found our forever place.

I totally get that you can do your online research and you can ask other people what they think, but the only way you can get a real feel for somewhere new is to go there.

Debbie Favell's circumstances meant she couldn't follow that advice and she says, 'We bought our house from 1,800 miles away without having set foot in it. We Googled the area we were moving to, to work out its locality to my husband's job, amenities, crime rate, schools, etc. We built a great relationship with the realtor so she could get an understanding of who we were, our wish list, budget and could effectively be our eyes on the ground, so to speak. The first time we had been to the province, city and our new home was when we drove up with the keys in hand fresh from the lawyer's office.'

With the above in mind, wherever possible, getting a feel for the place at all times of the day, in all seasons, and working out the culture, diversity and general feel should be factored in to your planning stage so you can be as confident as possible that you're doing the right thing and moving to the right place.

Francesca Aaen and her family moved to Andorra from Scotland in 2018, and says, 'We came once in summer and once in winter for holidays. Once we had decided, we came out twice to visit schools and look at apartments. We love it here now and we've created a really nice life for ourselves, made friends with some really interesting people and had opportunities we would never have had in the UK.'

Visits are fun, but they're fact-finding missions to help you get to grips with the good, the bad and the downright blinking ugly of somewhere new.

Once you've moved you can take your time to go to the hot spots, but these visits are a fundamental part of relocating the successful way, so put in the time and do the groundwork, to confirm you're on the right lines of where to move to.

Stay Where You're Thinking of Moving To

It wasn't swanky, but when we were on trips to Devon, our base was a Premier Inn in Newton Abbot – clean, cheap and the beds were new! We don't live in that town, but it was a base from which to explore, and, after the first visit, we knew it wasn't the place for us to live, but we did find a village along the coast road that was. You really need to be exposed to the area you're thinking of moving to as much as possible so you can know what will work for you in the long term. Staying at the Ritz to explore Hertfordshire probably won't work, but staying at a B&B in Hemel Hempstead would be a good starting point. This approach means you can get a feel for not just the city, town or village you want to live in, but also the roads within those places.

Talk to People

If you're brave enough, talking to people in the local area about their experiences of living where you're thinking of moving to can be really helpful. Yes, you can look online and read comments on forums, but you get so much from being there in real life. The woman on the checkout at Waitrose, the barista in the local coffee shop, the estate agents, librarians and bus drivers are the ones who will be honest, and let's face it, that's what you need if your relocation is going to be a success.

I remember being in Teignmouth when we first entertained the idea of living by the sea, and I asked a woman sitting outside Costa what her thoughts about schools were. Not only did she sing the praises of her children's school, but her openness and willingness to help me – a complete stranger – were confirmation that this could be a place for us to live, a community to be a part of and somewhere our children could thrive.

Talking to people not only gives you a glimpse into their world, but it can be an indication of just how friendly the locals are, how welcoming the community will be and whether you think it would be a place where you could feel at home. Don't bombard them with personal questions, but if you can strike up conversations, you'll be amazed at the gems of information that come to the surface as you chat, and the friendships that may well follow.

What's Going On?

When you visit somewhere, be aware of what's going on around you. Are there lots of empty shops or is the high street full of shoppers, with cafés on kerb sides and a library that's well stocked with books? Are there plans for a new hospital or GP surgery? Is a train link being planned that will make getting into London faster? Are there plenty of for-sale boards up as you drive through the roads you're interested in living on? You might not be looking to move somewhere hip and trendy, it's just worth noting the kinds of shops around you, whether there are business parks full of commerce and if the schools look smart, as these factors can indicate whether somewhere is up and coming or going down the pan.

Traffic Jams and Public Transport

On the first day at school in Devon, we took the 'back route', expecting the traffic to be horrendous, but we arrived early without even a tractor to hold us up. Fast-forward five years and the traffic is awful, to the point that I want to move closer to school – we are only ten miles away. We also live near a school, not our school, and this adds to the stress in my life because as pupils have increased so have the number of parents who park across our drive and generally drive me mad. I strongly suggest that when you visit somewhere new, you pay attention to the state of the traffic. Where are the hot spots? Which roads will you need to use to get to work? Are there plans for major roadworks, or building projects, that could impact your life after the move?

If you're using public transport – maybe you're moving out of London to Gerrards Cross, but need to get to your city office – how good are the trains, what does a season ticket cost, and if you visit and check the car park at 7.30 a.m., will you even be able to park there? If you have children, is there a decent bus or train service that will give them the independence to see friends as they get older, and are they able to walk or cycle to school, or will you become a minibus service for the next few years?

I know this might sound over the top, but these are the kinds of details that can really impact how successful your relocation turns out. While things change – who knew we would see a global pandemic in 2020 that sent people hurtling to move to Devon faster than you could say 'vaccine' – scoping these things out now could save you time, energy and a kidney infection (true story) further down the line. You could, if you really wanted to, set traffic updates while you visit just to see if there are any common patterns that could make the road you have set your heart on living in impractical.

Live Like a Local

You might not feel like a local, but living like one when you visit is a good way to work out if somewhere new is right for you. I'm not saying you need to organise for Amazon to deliver books to your Airbnb or do a full supermarket shop just because that's what you do on Sunday, but if you can look at the way you generally run your life, and add that into the mix at this point, it could be beneficial.

The thing with relocating is that while it's very exciting and you have much to look forward to, when you arrive you're still going to have to run errands, put the bins out and go to the doctors.

With this in mind, look at how many coffee shops there are (I still miss being able to walk to Starbucks, but I don't miss the snotty woman I had to regularly pass to get there). Can you get your nails done? What about a hairdresser who can do a decent set of highlights? Is there a good Indian takeaway? Go see.

Where is the library, or is there a mobile van that visits once a month like ours? Is there a cinema on the doorstep? We have to drive at least 15 miles to watch anything on the big screen. The same goes for bowling, but we can walk to the beach and there are outdoor lidos aplenty on our doorstep. When you go somewhere new, just think about what you normally do, and while you might make life changes as part of a relocation, if having a golf club, yoga studio or independent brewery nearby is important to you, suss this out now.

You might find there is a tourist information office or a local museum, and they are fantastic places to go to get a feel for what's happening where you want to be.

PS Living like a local doesn't mean wearing a Barbour jacket, Joules T-shirt and Hunter wellies all at the same time as you traipse around penny arcades on the north Cornwall coast!

Watch the Weather

You can watch the forecast and check the meteorological apps on your phone all you like, but actually noticing what the weather does when you're visiting somewhere new can help you make the right decision for you. My dad lives by the sea in Norfolk and while they don't get a lot of rain, in the winter it's really cold and there's a vicious wind that rolls in from the North Sea. I know that location wouldn't work for me, as our winters tend to be mild, even if they are on the soggy side.

The weather doesn't have to be a make-or-break for you, and the climate could be one of the reasons why you're moving, but just check in and see what's going on to make sure it fits with your idea of a good life.

If Your Relocation Is Abroad

When I think about relocating to Tokyo at twenty-two, on my own and with the internet not even a thing, I'm not quite sure how I did it, but not overthinking it came into play. I was young, ambitious and not ready to be chained to a desk, so I headed to the Land of the Rising Sun with pretty much zero planning, a suitcase, a rucksack and a broken heart to heal.

Now, while it worked for me back when I was young, free and single, I'm not sure that a 'suck it and see' approach is one I'd suggest, especially if you and your family have a lot riding on your move.

Leaving one country for another is pretty huge, but it's also exciting, liberating and an amazing opportunity to be brave and live a life you love. However, to make the transition as smooth as possible, and to prepare for success from the start, it's wise to do your research and get a handle of just how this is going to work out for you.

Charlie Lemmer has moved internationally a number of times and has some super-helpful tips that could make the transition a success for you.

Always learn a little bit of the language before you arrive

Even if it's just a few phrases to get you by at the beginning, not only does it help you settle in with the locals, but it's extremely stressful, costly and annoying when you come home from the shop with yogurt instead of milk, for the third time in a row!

Don't be cheap

If you think because you've backpacked around the world that you can navigate the bureaucratic system in a new country with ease, think again. Moving is stressful enough as it is; don't do it to yourself. It's well worth using either a full-on relocation agent if you have a family, or an expert like Just Landed (https://www.justlanded.com/) – for a small fee they will get you all the appointments for the necessary paperwork and meetings to get you through all the hurdles to make you legal. They understand the system and know all the back doors so it's money well spent.

Visit the embassy of the country you're moving to in the UK before travelling

I did this before moving to Spain and managed to set up the ID number I needed to open bank accounts and rent property before I even landed on the tarmac. This saved me so much time and stress.

Know the law, rules and customs before you go

When I relocated to Dubai I met countless people who didn't even know the country was Muslim – or maybe they did but they had no respect for the culture and were constantly being arrested for behaving illegally. There are severe punishments for obvious things like drugs, but lesser-known rules can get you into serious trouble, too. Financial crime there is taken very seriously: bouncing a cheque was illegal, for example (yes it was a while ago).

Also, I didn't know, for example, that it's illegal to share a flat or house with anyone of the opposite sex without being married. Point being: do your homework.

Join the relevant Facebook group for where you're going

There is always a local expat group with thousands of helpful people on it that is full of great info – from where to buy the favourite jam that reminds you of home to contacts for pet sitters – and I have always found this a valuable tool everywhere I have moved.

Bringing all of this together, Phil Leivesley says, 'Before relocating to a completely new area, do your homework and find out as much as you can about the location. Where are the nice bits and the not-so-nice bits? What are the local schools like and what sort of transport links are available? What is the air quality like and how busy is the traffic? Is the area too busy or too quiet for you? Does it suit the lifestyle choice you'd like to make? What about your work situation? Can you work from home, and would you be able to keep doing so if you were to change jobs? Is it practical and sensible for you to live there? Do you know anyone in the area who can give you useful local knowledge?'

Relocation exercise

As you scope out somewhere new, keep a note of whether that location is really going to work for you and make your relocation a success.

Ask yourself:

- Are the people friendly?
- Is there a diverse mix of people?
- Are the roads busy, the car parks full and do people clean up after their dogs?
- How close are the schools to where we want to live?
- What are the shops like?
- Are there leisure facilities?
- Does it feel like home?

Chapter Five

Wherever I Lay My Hat...

Congratulations!

You're really clear on *why* you're relocating. You've also decided *where* you want to relocate to. You've visited your preferred location, at least once, and the next considerations are: what are you going to do with your current home and what will your next one look like?

One of my all-time favourite websites is Rightmove, whether I'm moving or not. Forget Asos, I love looking at houses, seeing what I could afford to buy – if I won the lottery – and planning my next home.

The potential of a blank canvas is so exciting, and I hope this is something you'll feel as you consider where you're going to set up home next.

Renting When You Move On?

I'm not talking about Macclesfield, Marbella or Maidenhead, but the bricks and mortar you call home, unless you live on a houseboat, and that's a whole different scenario.

Whether you're currently renting or are a homeowner, you'll need to decide what happens with your current abode.

If you're a tenant, and you're moving on to pastures new, this can be an easier option, but you'll need to look at your contract to find out what notice period you have to give, and how you're most likely to get your deposit back. Your landlord shouldn't charge you for the normal wear and tear associated with a rental, but getting all your cash returned can be hard, so make sure you follow their criteria when leaving. This will potentially include a deep clean of the property (possibly by a professional, with an invoice as proof), tidying up the garden, emptying the bins, as well as handing back the correct number of keys and any paperwork connected to your time living there.

Before you move out, double check all cupboards, the loft and garage for possessions; and the packing tips later on in this chapter will help ensure a tidy departure. Oh, and if an inventory is needed, ensure you do it. Make sure your rent has been paid up to date, that all utility bills have been paid in full, and redirect your post because you don't want your sensitive mail falling into the wrong hands.

Taking photos of the gas and electricity meters, and having images of the property before you close the door for the last time is a good idea. Keeping copies of emails you sent about issues (especially those that weren't dealt with) is further insurance that you've done all that was expected and should have your deposit back in your account, which is cash that'll help your relocation be a success.

It's worth noting that you might have to show prospective tenants around for your landlord, something else to check in your contract. While this can be annoying and eat into your time when you have so many other things to do, smile and be as helpful as you can. Your landlord should give you notice before anyone comes to look at the property, and people shouldn't just turn up and expect to look around – that includes said landlord.

You might not own this place, but it's been your home and responsibility, so please have some regard to how you hand it back – let's call it good karma for your next step.

Homeowners: the Choices

For homeowners looking to relocate, you have two options: rent out your property or sell it. Each one comes with its own set of pros and cons, as well as a side serving of stress, but only you can decide what's going to work for you.

Renting out your place

If you're going to let your home out, you'll need to make sure you address any problems before it's listed, decide on whether you want to offer it furnished or unfurnished, as well as ensure it's clean and habitable. You'll also need to look at what the rent is going to be. All of this can be hard work, but it means having an income (depending on what you rent at the other end) as well as a nest egg for the future, and, if things don't go to plan, you have somewhere to return to.

My main suggestion is that you use a lettings or management agency as this can save you time, energy and, in the long run, money. Yes, you can keep your Fulham flat and rent it out to a couple for hundreds a month, but if the pipes burst or the heating breaks down, you're not going to want to jump on the red eye from New York to sort it out. It was for this reason we didn't rent out our last house. While we could have used a management agency, the idea of spending weekends on the congested M5 to sort out radiators in the suburbs, when we could have been paddleboarding in Salcombe, didn't appeal.

If you're in two minds about renting out or selling up, maybe draw up a list of pros and cons, but also go with your intuition; it can be helpful to do that from time to time!

Ben Small, CeMAP, a mortgage and protection adviser, has thoughts on this and says, 'If you fancy keeping your own home, you could look at a Let to Buy mortgage. This is when the lender changes your mortgage to allow you to rent your old home so that it frees up your affordability to buy a new home. For example, if you own a home and are paying your mortgage, this money is not being replenished, meaning if you were to buy another house a lender would see the new mortgage as an extra cost. However, if you were to convert where you lived into a rental, the income received would offset this cost, freeing up your income for your new mortgage. When reviewing this option, it's best to speak with a professional as each lender has different criteria, and usually requires a 25 per cent deposit/equity in your property.'

If selling is right for you, skip to the next step, but if you decide to rent, you need to find the right agency, to give you peace of mind that, when you're in pastures new, not only will they find tenants, but they will look after them and your property so you don't have to worry. Yes, it costs, but it's worth it.

With all of this, start your research early, ask for recommendations, get contracts in place, meet tenants if you feel better about knowing who will be in your home and put a timeline in place. While it's not a case of washing your hands of things altogether, having them take over could be an investment that helps you successfully settle somewhere new.

Selling up when you ship out

Okay, this is the biggie. As much as I love moving, I hate selling houses, but it's a necessary evil, so let's help you to get it right.

Once you have decided to sell, before you do anything else, make a list of the jobs you need to do to be sale-ready. From painting the downstairs loo and mending the back fence to finally fixing that dodgy garage door and clearing out the front garden, list them down and get on with it. Have a timeframe in place and get to work, drafting in tradespeople if needed, because if you don't, surveyors will flag up anything that's wrong, and that could hold up your sale further down the line and even cost you a buyer.

You don't have to do every last thing, but get your house looking as good as you can, so you feel proud when the for-sale board goes up, not slightly embarrassed at what people will find when they step inside the front door.

Finding an estate agent

They tend to get a bad rap, but a good estate agent won't just help you to sell your home, they'll help you decide the best price, and get it, as well as support you during the process. Ask around for recommendations, speak to a few different agents and look at their offerings and prices. Yes, you can do it yourself, but the question is: do you want to?

Katie Griffin, owner and director of estate agents Sawdye & Harris, knows selling your home is one of the biggest financial transactions you're ever likely to make. It could be an emotional time for you, so she has some key questions to help you choose the right estate agent for you.

Before you speak to an agent, be clear on your plans as this is often how they will start a discussion. Make sure you're clear on why you're selling and what kind of timescale you're working towards. If you're going to buy something else, write a list of your needs and wants. The agents you speak to about selling will also be keen to show you what great homes they have on their books, and you'll get a feel for how they deal with prospective buyers.

Do your homework
How good is their website? Is it professional-looking, can you navigate it easily and has it got all the main information you want to know? Are you impressed by the look of their listings?

Are they a member of a professional body?
Agents who are members are bound to work to the highest professional standards and adhere to a strict code of conduct. This isn't to say that agents who aren't members don't work to the same level, it's just good to know and allows you to make an informed decision – get the full picture before you make your choice.

Are their homes listed on the best portals?
There are plenty of sales websites out there that have a far wider reach than an agent's site alone. The more popular sites an agent lists your home on, the more prospective buyers will see your home. There are several popular portals agents can use, so ask them which ones they use, and why.

Have they got homes for sale that are similar to yours?
You might think having competition is a disadvantage, but actually it can be a good sign that the agent is used to marketing your type of home to the right kind of buyer.

When the agent comes to your home for a valuation, or when you speak to them directly, ask: 'What's the market like at the moment?' Their answer will give you an idea of how many viewings you're likely to get and how long it might take to sell.

You'll also get a feel for how knowledgeable the agent is.

Asking 'What similar homes have you sold recently?' will confirm what kind of sale price is possible. And if the agent has sold several properties like yours in the last month or so, it shows the market is buoyant and they're doing a pretty good job.

'How much would you market our home for?' is another question to ask them. You'll probably already have an idea of this from looking online, so compare that with what the agent says, and see how confident they are when they give you their valuation. They'll usually state a range and then recommend an initial market price based on your own timescale and situation. If that's different to what you thought, don't be afraid to ask more questions and discuss it further.

Ask, 'Do you have any potential buyers in mind?' Of course they're going to say yes, so follow it up by asking what those buyers have looked at recently and what their feedback has been. That will show you how engaged the agent is with buyers and how good they are at communicating.

It might feel hard, but asking 'What happens if I'm not happy with the service?' is within your rights. As long as you've chosen your agent carefully, you shouldn't have any real issues, but it's always a good idea to check what the minimum contract period is, and how much notice you need to give.

Once you've found two or three agents you're sure can do the job, based on the above, it's time to turn to the bonus question: Which agent feels right? Putting it simply, who do you like best? Due diligence plus gut feeling is a tried and tested formula that works for so much in life, and in this case, it should give you the best-selling partner and a successful sale.

Think about the photos

The right estate agent will also help with the photos. Poppy Jakes is a photographer and has some simple, effective tips to help you get things right:

- Less is more when it comes to photos, so declutter as much as you can and dress your house for the photos, as well as for selling. This could be with soft furnishings, fresh flowers, or you can even set the table, so it gives the buyer a feel of the house being more of a home.
- When taking photographs of your home, always use a tripod, make sure your camera is level, and at chest height. You want people to feel like they are in the room experiencing it for themselves, but if the camera is too high or too low that intimate feeling is lost.
- Using a wide-angle lens is critical and shooting in landscape is required by most websites. Buyers want to see the size of the rooms, but, equally, detailed shots of interesting parts of the property will give buyers more of an idea of the space, and whether it's somewhere they might want to live, or at least view.
- Just as when people come to look at your property, when the photos are taken, make sure you have the curtains open as wide as possible to let all the natural light in, and pop on all side lights to give the rooms softness and warmth.

When it comes to showing people around your home, or your estate agent doing their job, you want to ensure it is styled and looks as appealing as possible. Yes, we know that it won't look like this all the time, but if you're serious about selling, you want to be as proactive as possible.

Boost kerb appeal
Now that the inside is sorted, if you're serious about selling, remember that potential buyers could have a sneaky drive-by to see your home. If it's not looking good, they might decide it's not worth a visit. I know people have done this to us and I also know we've done it when we've been looking to move and driven away. If there's a tonne of junk in the front garden, a broken window or the neighbourhood kids are camping out in the street, we haven't been impressed. Sad, but true. While you

can't tell the peeps next door to clear up, you can take care of your own shop window, and I'd suggest you do this. A freshly painted front door, neat front garden, cut grass, working gates, lights, bins stored away, and cars parked in the drive, or mindfully on the road, will help make that all-important first impression a good one.

Planning and dealing with viewings

One tip is to make sure your agent gives you advance notice for viewings, but if you really want to sell, be flexible and try to keep your home tidy so you can accommodate potential purchasers. I've had to get houses ready to be viewed when I've been ill, pregnant, looking after a child in a cast, as well as being on a work deadline, but it was always worth it, because I had my eye on the prize – my next home.

I remember having a call from an estate agent while on a train coming home from a long day of meetings in London, to say a celebrity wanted to look at our house the next morning! The heels came off as soon as I got home, the rubber gloves went on and while dinner cooked, we set to work ensuring we presented a palace fit for a pop princess.

We pretended we didn't know she was famous when she knocked at the door, acted cool, and whilst she didn't put in an offer, the next day someone else did, so the cleaning frenzy was worth it.

Of course, your agent can show people around for you, which is great if you're out at work or busy with your move, but as a seasoned mover, I was happy to do this, and it meant I could answer questions on the spot.

Good luck!

Where Are You Going Next?

So, you've got a plan of what to do with your current home, but where are you going to live next? Home is very much where the heart is, so whether you decide to rent, buy or hop from one Airbnb to another, you need to find the right place for now, if you want your relocation to be successful in the long term.

The British have a preoccupation with owning their own home, but renting when you relocate can be a great idea. Not only does it take away some of the pressure to complete your purchase within a slim timeframe, but it also gives you an initial base from which to explore when you arrive.

If you're a homeowner, renting can add to the bottom line of your move, especially if there's a period when you don't have tenants. It can, however, help make things a success, so it's absolutely worth considering. You might just want to get settled and close the door on what was, but while renting can add extra work, costs and stress, it takes off some of the pressure when it comes to finding that forever home, which for some strange reason never seems to be on the market when you want to buy it – how is that?

By renting you can take off some of the time pressures to get your children into the school you know is perfect for them if nothing right is for sale in the location. You need an address to get a place, and if your house isn't selling, it might be that renting will get you the education spot for the new term, but without having to complete a sale and purchase.

Renting also means it's less likely you'll have to lower your sale price because you're desperate to secure a buyer, which happens when people are working to tight deadlines. At the same time, you won't feel like you have to buy a property that isn't right. When we came to Devon we rented for the first eight months; some of that was due to the outcome of the referendum to leave the EU and the market flattened for a while, but it meant we were able to get a feel for the area and work out where we wanted to live. I can't actually see the waves from my bedroom window, despite being able to get to the water in five minutes, so I know one day we will move again, but it worked out well for us because we had extra time to play with.

When Lucy Davies moved out of London she rented for two years, and says, 'I rented at first, while I established myself, and then bought a house. It was great to have a semi-permanent home for a while, so that I could work out exactly where I wanted to live.'

Renting is a fantastic option when you move abroad as Francesca Aaen, who moved to Andorra in 2018, found out. 'We are still renting in 2021. We rented out our house in the UK, so we had somewhere to go back to – we have just sold it as we're going to stay here for the next chapter!'

She isn't alone. Debbie Favell told me about her experiences when she moved to Canada, and says, 'I found a company in our original city that had a group of properties that were available to rent on a weekly basis (a little like Airbnb). This meant that we had a fully furnished property to call home for six weeks when we arrived from England, and this allowed us time to research what area of the city we wanted to live in and find a rental property there. After the initial six-week property, we rented a local house for about eighteen months. We didn't look to buy a house in Saskatoon as there was an internal transfer for my husband to a different province (Ontario). We have bought a house here in Ontario now.'

Leah Eser summarises by saying, 'My first relocation was with my employer, so they put me in accommodation for the first two weeks whilst I looked for my own place. Singapore is extremely expensive, so there was no way I was able to afford a place of my own. My first place I rented a room in an apartment with two other guys, but it had a serious cockroach infestation and I had to get out! I then rented an apartment with my friend from work and when she moved in with her boyfriend, I found a room to rent with two other British girls. Then, when I moved to San Francisco to be with my husband, he was renting a room, so we stayed there for a bit until I got a job, and we could afford our own place. We now rent our apartment in the San Francisco Bay (we LOVE it), and we are looking to buy.'

I know I've emphasised the need to visit new locations as much as you can, but in some cases that's simply not possible. Renting means you haven't made a huge financial investment in a town that isn't for you after all.

Jo Henderson moved on a relocation contract with her husband's work, and she says, 'We had the opportunity to move out to the US full time, but we'd no longer have our rent paid and it was then we had to make the decision whether we stayed out there and sold up in the UK or came home. We decided to come home. The first time we had no base to come back to and that was one of the hardest things – we left London, moved to LA and when we came back, we weren't sure we wanted to move back to our old life. We ended up moving to Bournemouth – but quickly realised that wasn't the right move, so ended up in London again.'

You might want to rush in and buy on day one, but renting gives you a flexible base from which you can start your relocation adventure. Make sure when you do buy your home, it will be a forever one, or at least be right for you for a few years.

Ben Small, CeMAP, talked to me about this and says, 'Buying vs. renting, when you move, is a question that comes up a lot, but it really depends on your situation and there are pros and cons to each argument. When you buy, you feel you haven't wasted any money on renting, you can make it your own home straight away, and you feel like you have not put an element of your life on hold. If you rent when you move, you're able to explore the area to find out where is best for you, it takes the rush out of getting a mortgage arranged, as it becomes two separate transactions: the sale, then the purchase. By separating the two transactions, it can also be less stressful. Lots of people are worried that they won't be able to get a mortgage if they've just changed jobs; for most lenders this is not a concern if you have changed recently, they are more concerned if you have taken a break in employment, normally more than six weeks.'

Buying Somewhere New

If you want to buy somewhere new (as in new for you, not necessarily a new-build), that's great and what a brilliant opportunity to make your relocation a real success.

Looking at online listings is one thing, but finding the right house is going to come down to what you want and need, and it might take more than one viewing to make up your mind.

Look at the things in a property you can't live without, as well as the things that would be nice but aren't deal-breakers.

- Is it in the right location? Be really, really honest here. We moved to the wrong town when we first left London and I hated it. Again, I'd say listen to your intuition, as well as paying attention to the figures and online details.
- Is it on a main road or a cut-through?
- Is it close to good schools, or the school you want your kids to go to? Or is it near a school where the parents will park on your drive. Avoid this at all costs.
- Is there a garage, drive or off-street parking?
- How many flights of stairs are there?
- Is there a garden, if you want one? Is there a pond, if you want one? Are there fences in place and decent gates? You don't want costs mounting up if work isn't complete.
- What does the area look like and what do the neighbours seem like? I know this is hard, but try to get a feel for this kind of thing as this could be where you live, so you want to feel comfortable and relaxed.
- How many bathrooms are there, and what state are they in?
- What's the kitchen like? Does it need a refit? Are there extractor fans? Is there mould? These are all costs you might not want to take on, so look out for them early on so you can query them.
- What state are the windows in? Will you need new double glazing?
- Is it a listed building? This can be hard work, so pay attention to the fine details.
- Are there any cracks in the walls?
- What condition are the floors in? You don't want to move into a house full of filthy carpets that need deep cleaning, or worse, totally replacing.

Relocation exercise

Buying a property isn't a matter to take lightly, so with every potential purchase have a checklist ready in your relocation journal and ask yourself the same set of questions for each place you look at.

Review your notes and make sure the home you're purchasing matches your needs and hopefully some of your wants, too.

Whether you're buying or renting, refer to your lists so you don't let your heart get carried away and end up with a property that's not going to work for you.

I'm not saying it has to be perfect, but getting most of the criteria right is more likely to lead to happiness. Being impulsive might mean you have a beautiful thatched cottage that looks gorgeous on the Gram, but if there's terrible damp in the bedrooms and your son has asthma, it's not going to make for a successful move.

Let's Move On

Congratulations, you've decided on your next property!

This is a really exciting time, but things could get stressful. Remember, you're in it for the long game, so don't quit now.

Waiting for your offer to be accepted, hoping you don't get gazumped, and the joy of packing and decluttering can take the shine off your relocation. However hard it feels, remember that it'll all be worth it when you get to your new home and can start the next chapter in your life.

Chapter Six

What's It Going to Cost?

One of the most common reasons people gave me for not making a big move when I was researching this book came down to cold hard cash – or the lack of it. Add to that stress and uncertainty, and you've got the perfect combination of pressure and doubt to keep you where you are: stuck.

I'm not going to lie, relocating is an expensive business, and it would be irresponsible for me to encourage you to do it if it was going to leave you in debt. So rather than painting an idyllic picture of life by the beach, only to dash your hopes further down the line when it becomes apparent you need to do some serious saving before you're anywhere close to the golden coast of Australia, I'm talking about it now.

I'm not saying you must put this book down if the numbers feel out of reach – please don't – but I want to be open and honest and say that if you want to relocate successfully, you need to know the costs involved. There's no precise figure, and that figurative piece of string is going to be long, but it's far better to get this bit out of the way, work out what you need in the bank, and then start to make progress towards your end goal of successfully relocating.

Costs before You Move

When we think about relocating, removal companies, bank charges and stamp duty come to mind, but there are many more costs to consider. I want to make sure that this chapter shows you what you're looking at when it comes to finances, and while I don't give figures (because they will vary so much for each reader and over time), I hope it will encourage you to plan and budget for your relocation so that it's a success.

Before we go any further, let's add the costs of visiting places you potentially want to move to and the research you will need to do. Petrol in the car to go from Amersham to Eastbourne, train tickets to Scotland or plane fares to Portugal, combined with hotels, pet sitters, insurance, restaurant bills and cocktails to celebrate signing on the dotted line will all add up. It's impossible to put a figure on how much this will be. One friend went to Lyme Regis once and bought a house when she was there, another went on holiday to Sweden three times before making up her mind, so it's going to be up to you, but just know you will need to pay for this.

Estate agent fees

Some people sell their property themselves, but, for most, an estate agent will do the work for you at a price. Costs are going to vary from place to place, and from property to property, so do some research, shop around, ask for recommendations and don't accept first prices: there could be room for flexibility.

Katie Griffin says, 'Most agents do an all-in fee, but some charge extra for things like glossy brochures, so make sure you're clear on all the costs. And remember that a good agent will give you value for money, so don't be tempted to go for the cheapest – you tend to get what you pay for!'

Stamp duty

In England and Northern Ireland, stamp duty is the tax you pay when you're buying a home. The amount payable depends on the cost of the property. In Scotland and Wales, you'll pay Land and Buildings Transaction Tax (LBTT), so factor this in or it'll be a nasty surprise at the checkout.

Mortgages

If you need a mortgage, you need to look at the costs carefully, because they are a serious commitment. You want to ensure you can afford to live where you want to go to, something people don't always consider.

Phil Leivesley, has a further valuable point to make when he says, 'When you're looking to move, make sure your dream location is affordable. Do your research on prices in the area where you'd like to live, make sure they are affordable and that you will be able to buy a property that compares to where you are now. Unless you intend to downsize, you may want the same amount of space. Have a good idea of what the typical price range is for the property you have in mind. While some of us dream of moving to the coast and tend to think we could save money if we move further out of the city, coastal towns can be deceptively expensive. It's also worth looking at how the cost of living in your desired area compares to where you are now.'

Valuations and surveys

What kind of property you're buying will determine the valuation and surveys you need, and the prices they incur will differ depending on the type of survey, valuation and property. Many lenders don't charge for valuations, but a survey is recommended. This is a specialist report by a RICS-qualified professional, preferably a chartered surveyor, that will either say you're good to go or highlight issues and problems with a property.

While having one done might add a few hundred pounds to your outgoings, it could save you from buying something that is falling down, full of asbestos or likely to need an expensive new roof the moment it starts to rain.

Oliver Trice is a RICS chartered surveyor, and says, 'While it's not a legal requirement to have a survey when buying a property, I'd say that in the majority of cases, it's worth it and makes long-term financial sense. Far from being an unnecessary cost, a survey is an invaluable investment that not only gives you peace of mind that your new home is safe and secure, but will prevent any nasty surprises when you move in. For example, a survey could identify rising damp, a leaking roof or poor electrics, which, if found once you move in, could cost a significant amount to put right. A new-build or very recently constructed property might not need a survey, but I would still suggest you have one carried out to check for post-construction problems. If it's an older property, a listed building, a house with a thatched roof or a building with complex boundaries or extensions, a survey by a suitably qualified surveyor is a must. The cost of a survey will be insignificant compared to the cost of a new roof. It might not reveal any major issues, but if it does, it could be the saving grace for your relocation success.'

Maintenance and repairs

Your survey should highlight any items that need fixing, and you may well have a list of your own, so make sure you have a pot of cash to do the work yourself or to pay for people to do the repairs for you.

This might sound scary, but having experts on your team to deal with the legalities of buying or selling a property is as priceless as it is pricy.

Asking family or friends for recommendations is a sure way of finding someone who will get this done and not stuff it up at the last hurdle – it's been known.

Insurance

Building, contents, life, pet and moving insurance are all available here, and you will be glad you took these out if something goes wrong, so do your research and don't scrimp, or you could be totally out of pocket.

Deposits

If you're sofa surfing, you won't need a deposit (but you will need to pitch in for bills and food); otherwise one will need to be paid. Whether it's required to secure the mortgage for your dream house in Shropshire or three months' rent on a condo in California, you'll need a pot of cash for this. You should set aside money for broker and admin costs. It goes without saying, the more you pay for somewhere to live, the bigger the deposit is going to be, unless you're paying the full sale price up front, so don't miss this step out as it could cost you a buyer or break your chain. You might also need to put down a deposit on a new car, for a nursery spot or a school place if you're paying for education, so check the T&Cs for details.

Cleaning up

This has been mentioned already, I know, but if you're renting, check what your tenancy agreement says about cleaning when you leave, as this could impact getting your deposit back. If it's your house, you'll want to leave it clean, I hope, and this might include paying someone else to spruce it up if you're running out of time to deal with it yourself.

Utilities

As well as taking meter readings, you'll need to pay off your electric, gas, council tax and water bills before you go, and possibly pay up front for new ones on arrival, so build this into your costs. It could also be that you will have final rent and mortgage payments, and new ones, so add these too and don't forget phones and broadband – they could be vital to a successful move.

Redirecting post

It's worth redirecting your post because, while it's another cost, you don't want to miss bills or important letters that could create problems for you if left unaddressed. You might not want anyone else opening up your mail either, so set this up before you go; you won't regret it.

Storage

If you're renting, or are going to be between homes for a period of time, you may need to pay for storage. You don't want to have to beg, borrow or steal garage space or cash from your mum and dad, and offloading a sofa and kitchen table on your bestie probably won't go down too well however much they love you.

Temporary accommodation

No matter how well you plan a move, things can go wrong, so if there is wiggle room to add money to cover unexpected delays and a few nights in a hotel or Airbnb, it's worth considering it.

Sleeping in your car won't be fun, and if you've got kids and pets they'll need a base, so just have this in the back of your mind for any worst-case scenarios.

On-the-day Costs

Removal company

You might pay your removal company in full before you move, but in any case you should add this into your costs, as well as a tip for the people who move you on the day. If you're moving yourself (brave, back-breaking, but cost-effective) look at the cost of hiring a van, whether you need insurance to drive it, how much the fuel will cost, as well as any boxes and tape you need to get your possessions packed up and ready to go. Just as with other service providers, getting recommendations from family and friends, or on local Facebook groups, is the way to go, and always ensure they have the right moving insurance.

Parking

In some places, unless you've been able to get a resident's permit, you might have to pay for parking. Have coins and cards at the ready so you don't get a fine from a warden and ruin your first day.

Drinks and snacks

If you're organised, you might make packed lunches and flasks of tea; if not, feeding you and your team of helpers could get costly – even more so if things overrun. Allocate a pot of cash for this and always have plenty of water and snacks with you during the move. You might think you'll cook in your kitchen on the first night, but be prepared to find a takeaway or restaurant and factor this in.

Keys and locks

This won't be relevant to everyone and it will be bad luck if you do need to get extra keys or call out a locksmith, but if it happens, it won't be cheap, so have this in mind.

Costs on Arrival

Have you ever watched the TV show where families spend a week in Australia, seeing whether surf and sunshine is for them after all? The crunch point often isn't being near the sea, but the cost of living if they do decide to relocate. This is something to be aware of from the start.

If you're relocating for work, talk to HR about your package, including a modified salary. If it's an independent move, you might want to do some research now before you head to a supermarket in Geneva only to realise how much every little bit does actually help, or you'll have to eat beans on toast or get a side job to pay the bills.

Yes, big cities like London, Paris and New York come with a higher price tag, but so do some smaller towns and leafy suburbs, and I am not just talking about the real-estate value. A friend recently came to Devon from Huddersfield and immediately noticed that the cost of living here is more expensive, something I also notice when I go back to London. Visiting is a great way to see how prices differ, be that a bus ticket, a pint of beer or a bag of apples, and while it might only be a pound or two here and there, that soon adds up and can make a massive difference in the success of your move.

You might also need to think about childcare costs, dog kennels, new school uniforms, gym memberships, commuting costs and coffees with new friends; all of which add up, but are easy to overlook. If you need extra furniture, money to refurbish the kitchen, replace windows or resurface the drive, look at what is needed straight away and what can wait, given the money that has already left your account.

Emergency fund

People say to save for a rainy day, and I'd suggest you do exactly this when you relocate. You simply do not know what could happen and a burst pipe, a smashed bottle of ketchup across a new white carpet or the car dying are all possible, so just be aware that fate can deal you a poor hand.

This is not an exhaustive list, and I hope it hasn't put you off, but money is key to relocation success and it's worth making sure you can afford to do it before you make costly mistakes that could set you back and leave you in debt.

A successful relocation isn't about perfection straight away; it's about the long term, so don't hit the John Lewis website and max out your credit card on day one. Take it a day at a time and, remember, just as you sell and give things away, others might do the same for you, so ask.

Relocation exercise

I'm a writer, not an accountant, and Word documents are my comfort zone, so I'm keeping this super simple. In your relocation journal, create a relocation spreadsheet (like the one below) to help you work out the costs for your move, adding things as you go.

Doing this will hopefully start to show you how much it's going to cost, and if you find you can't make this work for your dream location, maybe a relocation rethink could help, or you could open a relocation bank account and start saving to make your dreams come true.

RELOCATION BUDGET			
COSTS BEFORE	COSTS DURING	COSTS AFTER	EMERGENCIES

Chapter Seven

Spilling the Beans

One of the hardest things about moving is telling people you're going, and having to say goodbye to those you love and who are part of your life at the moment. Relocating may well make your heart sing and your pulse quicken, but there's a very real chance that not everyone will be happy about your choice to move, and you need to be prepared for that.

It's impossible to predict how others will receive your news. Some will feel happiness, pride and joy, but for others, it could be that anger, confusion and betrayal are on the cards.

Michael Padraig Acton, bestselling author of *Learning How to Leave* and *Raw Facts from Real Parents*, told me how you can start to deal with the opinions of family and friends who don't want you to move: 'It's important to listen to those that really care for you and love you. Remind yourself, if you're moving, you're moving for an important reason. We don't just move because today is Tuesday. We move for a reason. So, remind people of the reasons you're moving, such as better lifestyle, job requirements, sick relatives, you want to try a rural location rather than an urban location, etc. Battle it out with them, do some work with them and maybe look through their Doubting Thomas eyes and ask, "What is the real reason you don't want me to move? I hear you challenging me but what's behind that? Let's be honest about our feelings and our thoughts? What is the real reason you're challenging me about moving?"

It's going to be impossible for you to control the reactions of others, and while you can consider what they say, please try not to let their feelings and opinions deter you from going or cloud your judgement. This is your life and your relocation to make work.

It doesn't matter how excited you are about the next step in your life, how amazing the job is, or how beautiful the mountain views from your kitchen in Switzerland are going to be, saying goodbye is hard. I remember the unexpected tears in the school playground when we left for Devon, and, yes, I still miss those friends and have a pang of sadness when I see photos on social media of them enjoying a night out at one of the local bars I used to visit with them.

Telling Family and Friends

'Surprise, we're moving to New Zealand!' might not be the words your nearest and dearest are expecting to hear at Sunday lunch, and their reactions could be as extreme as your relocation, so when, where and how you deliver the news of your departure needs to be sensitively planned, however excited you are.

There are no hard rules about who to tell and when, but I imagine for many people parents, siblings, older children, extended family members and close friends will be the first to know that change is afoot.

You'll have a different set of people to tell from anyone else reading this book, and some dynamics will be more complex than others; however, honesty and transparency are key to the smoothest process.

If you have even an inkling that heading to Paris to take up that dream job will upset your mum and dad, cause your granny to miss you and leave your mates miffed, then be prepared for their reaction. Make sure the time and place for spilling the beans feels right – or as right as it can be – and that will help ease things for all parties.

There are those who are super sensitive who will sulk, as well as people who are prone to angry outbursts, so working out the best way to communicate your needs will be key to containing any negative fallout. Telling them about your dream move to Montreal at a birthday party or in a packed pub might not be your best plan.

Keeping the news secret could offend those closest to you by making them feel left in the dark. If someone feels like they're the last to know, or they've been lied to, it could potentially add an extra layer of disappointment and resentment, which is natural but not pleasant to deal with for either party.

Michael Padraig Acton suggests looking at what you can do to help others – and yourself – with the transition of moving away. He says, 'Today we have Facetime, Skype, Zoom, cheaper travel, all sorts of things. If it's doable then we can start new family traditions or new friendship traditions where we meet every Easter or halfway, or we could say, "We're going to make more effort and do this." Make it into a positive. Find a way that you can establish new traditions or new ways of communicating, new ways of being.'

Give Them Advance Warning

Sharing your moving plans will not only give your loved ones time to process the news, but it will also give you a handful of people you can confide in before the move. Doing this means you can get them involved in your plans – maybe they'll want to visit with you one weekend when you're house hunting – and it gives you someone to talk to if you're having a wobble (pick that person carefully). It also means you can plan to do fun things together before you go.

In some cases you don't get months and months to plan a relocation; but giving people the most time you can could be the best leaving present of all.

Avoid Making Online Announcements before Telling Those Who Need to Know

As I was mentally packing to live by the sea, I was also dying to share our plans with the world, but I held back. It was really hard, but if you don't want to land in hot water I suggest you don't post the news of your move on social media before telling those closest to you.

If your loved ones find out about the move via an online announcement before hearing from you directly, they will almost certainly be upset and offended – and who could blame them? While there's nothing wrong with an excited post on Facebook about your move to France to take over a vineyard, this can wait until you've shared the news with people you need to tell directly. It will prevent hurting feelings and damaging your relationships before you go.

The main thing to remember is that their reaction might not be one you want, but it shows they care. Yes, in some cases people will be trying to change your mind and manipulate you into staying, but that's because they'll miss you. If you've done all of the hard work and are making a move that's right for you, don't let their reaction stop you from achieving the success you deserve. Give them the time they need when it comes to telling them you're going, but try not to be swayed.

It's Them, Not You

This is a total cliché, but if people react negatively to your news, please remember it's more about their issues than yours. Ask yourself why they've responded in that way. Is it because they are too scared to take a chance to move somewhere new? Are they stuck in a rut and wish they could be as brave as you and make a change? Maybe they have a strong feeling of duty and wouldn't dare to move away from their mum and dad for fear of judgement? Whatever it might be, their reaction is theirs to feel, but it shouldn't impact on your dreams and goals. Hopefully, as time moves on, they will come to terms with the fact you have gone and, who knows, maybe you'll inspire them to make the changes they know they need to make.

Promise to Keep in Touch

I know you'll do this, but letting those closest to you know you'll stay in touch with them may put their minds at ease when it comes to you not being a part of their lives in the way you have been, up until now. Making phone calls, sending texts, checking Facebook and planning return visits makes maintaining connections easier, and if you want to make it work, you'll both put in the time and effort.

Over the years, people have come and gone in my life depending on where I've lived. For example, given there was no social media when I lived in Tokyo, keeping in touch with fellow teachers and flatmates from there has been pretty difficult, but that would be totally different had I been teaching there today. Some of the friends I had before we moved to Devon have disappeared over time, but some I worked with in London at the start of my career often pop into my DMs for old times' sake. At the end of the day, we find ways to keep close to those we truly want to maintain a relationship with. Relocating doesn't mean we don't like them and don't want to be friends with them any more; it's just that meeting for a coffee after the school run or going to a yoga class isn't as easy if you don't live in the same town.

As Jo Henderson, who moved from the UK to LA with her husband and two children, says, 'We made much more effort to stay connected because we were so far away. We did regular FaceTime and WhatsApp calls to parents and grandparents. My mum jokes that she saw more of us when we lived 5,000 miles away than when we lived down the road.'

Leah Eser adds, 'When it comes to friends, I would say that moving away makes quality over quantity really clear. There are very close friends I've stayed very close with, despite not seeing them for years, and when I've gone home it's like nothing has changed. There are others I don't speak to that much any more, and that's okay. I think there are some people who don't understand why I wouldn't go home, or why I'd want to live away. I used to try and justify myself, but I don't any more.'

You can't expect to stay in touch with everybody, and some people will drop off the radar, but those who matter will always matter, and you will communicate with them even if it takes effort and work! Neither my best friend from sixth form nor my roomie from uni are fans of social media, but we've kept in touch with each other for over thirty years, which is testament to the fact that those who matter, well, they really do matter.

Tell Your Boss and Colleagues Too

I talk about work and relocations in Chapter Nine, but if you work with other people, or have clients as a business owner, this is another potentially tricky situation you're going to have to navigate.

If you're relocating because of your job, people are going to know why your desk is looking slightly bare and your boss will be in the loop so they will hopefully help make the transition easy. If you're moving and they don't know, they'll need to.

If you're employed by someone else, this is the time to look at your notice period. For some of you there will be a three-month notice period, especially if you're in a senior role, for others it will be a month, two weeks or even a week, depending on what you do and who you work for.

Once you know what you're dealing with, rather than skulking around, it's best to be honest as soon as appropriate. Doing this will give them time to plan for your departure, and means you can be more open about what's happening for you, why you might need to take the odd Friday off here and there, and why there's a 'for sale' board outside your house. To make the transition as easy as possible, offer to assist with interviewing and/or training your replacement. By being affable and flexible, hopefully they will give you a good send-off as well as offering glowing references to your new boss.

If you work for yourself and your clients are location-dependent – maybe you're an electrician, a personal trainer or have a bricks-and-mortar shop – let them know your plans. If you have a good relationship with them and they're happy with your work, they could be upset and feel that you're letting them down, but giving them plenty of time, having recommendations of other people they can work with and not just dropping them at the last minute will go a long way towards softening the blow.

It's Not What You Say, It's the Way That You Say It

Like so many things, the way you tell those close to you about your plans can impact the way they respond to the news. If you position it as a really positive move for all of you – that there'll be a spare room with their name on it; that they can come for a holiday or visit for Christmas; that there are plenty of fun things to do in your new location and you know they'll love it as much as you – then you're already selling them your dream. By painting a picture of an exciting adventure, it's much harder for others to be openly negative. Inside, they might feel sad about you moving away, but your positivity will be infectious, and they'll want to see you fulfil your dream.

Throw a Party to Say Goodbye

Once the dust has settled and most people are either happy for you or understand why you're making such drastic changes, it's time to consider a goodbye party.

Some people choose to slip away quietly, especially if the move hasn't been embraced by others, but if that isn't you and you have the support and encouragement of family and friends, a party is a brilliant way to go out on a high. A party is a perfect way to say goodbye personally to those who've been a part of your life at your current location. It's also a brilliant way to signal change and to celebrate your new adventure, rather than hiding it under the carpet and shuffling away as if you're the bad guy in all of this.

For some people, this won't be a time when they want to throw on their glad rags, pop corks and wish you all the best, but for those who love and support you, and who can see why you're making this massive life decision, they will want what is best for you and a party is the perfect way to have a final night of fun!

Relocation Exercise
Take photos of family and friends before you leave and make them into a montage you can put in a frame and add to a wall in your new home. Send copies to family and friends as a parting gift.

Chapter Eight

Let's Talk About the Kids

Not every reader of this book will be moving with children, but if you are, it can be hard terrain to navigate, whatever age they are.

Even if your relocation is a positive thing for you and your kids, because it offers a better quality of life, better opportunities and maybe more sunshine, uprooting them from their home, friends, family and comfort zone could leave you wondering just why you're doing it.

What I'll say is that it's important to keep the faith, go back to your reason for the move and remember you're the adult in this scenario – even if there are times when you want to slam doors and shut yourself away with a massive bar of chocolate to binge watch Netflix. You can do this, and one day they may well thank you for taking the brave decision to create a better life for them.

I really believe that keeping kids in the loop when you're making a move is important. Of course, the level of involvement depends on their age – your one-year-old isn't going to want to consult Google Maps to work out the proximity of the closest park to your new home. But those who are a little older need to be involved, so don't keep them in the dark.

Michael Padraig Acton agrees it can be tough and says, 'Being honest and looking at pros and cons, pluses and minuses, is very important. If you explain the real reason why you're moving – whether it's a good or not such a good reason – children can manage this truth and work with it. Only give them as much truth as they can comprehend, for sure, but be honest with them. And then look at all the good things that we can hold on to with the new move.'

Being told you're moving can bring up a whole host of emotions.

Your children may feel they have no control over their lives, so bear this in mind as you go through the process. Let them know their emotions matter, that their concerns are important.

Siân Smith, an English teacher in Romania, says: 'The best thing a parent can do to prepare their children for change is to consult them at every stage of the process: from the point at which they're considering relocating, all the way to the actual move. Children and young people should never be underestimated, and their mental health can be fragile. Collaborating with them about major life changes can prevent them from feeling excluded, not having a voice, being overlooked and generally suffering from avoidable anxiety and/or depression.

'During this process, the reasons for a potential move should be outlined to a child and the obvious benefits and advantages of this should be discussed. For example, a better work–life balance, a better climate, better opportunities, a more advantageous educational path, better value for money, work commitments, promotion and so forth. Benefits such as access to open space, a better outdoor lifestyle, proximity to the beach and greater opportunities for extracurricular activities and clubs should be explored. Parents should actively show their children this online, with lots of forward planning so that they can research and analyse potential areas to live in, view potential houses, apartments and rentals; look at the geographical closeness of visitor attractions, outdoor landmarks and beaches, schools, leisure centres, shopping centres and what not. This would help to ease the anxiety of the unknown, and even make the change seem exciting – a goal to reach and something to look forward to.'

While your children can't put a stop to your move, they might try if they think you're 'ruining their lives', so it's important to tell them as soon as you can. I promise you, it's so much better for it to come from you, in a planned, constructive way, rather than for them to hear whispered conversations with estate agents, or find out from a friend whose mum saw it on Facebook.

When to Break the News

It could be that you've been thinking about a big move for a while, maybe all your life, but if it's not been on your kids' radar, it could feel like a massive blow and an adventure they don't want to be a part of. There might not be the perfect time or place to do this, but you don't want it to feel like a bolt from the blue for them. It doesn't have to be a massive meeting, just think about how you tell them and make sure you're around to answer questions and concerns, but don't press this if they don't want to talk about it.

Maybe you could cook their favourite dinner and talk about it over pizza in your cosy kitchen. You might be into walking as a family and you could broach it as you explore the woods, or perhaps as you hunker down with hot chocolate and a movie. Don't do it when you're under pressure to get out of the door to go to swimming lessons, or before people arrive for a BBQ and you have to answer the door with a tear-stained face and Dua Lipa blaring from a locked bedroom, but instead when you have the time and space to get it right.

Jai Fagan put this perfectly: 'When we relocated to New Zealand the children were only two and four, and I don't remember having a specific conversation with them about it, just that we were going to New Zealand "for a bit". When it came to coming back, seven years later, it was a family decision. We talked about it more than once. We didn't make lists or try to weigh up which place was better; we accepted they are just different and there would be a payoff either way. Eventually we went for lunch at our favourite café, and I took my laptop. I showed them our house in the UK, we looked at what school they would go to, we did a Google Maps walk around the city and made a list of things we wanted to do if we moved back. We were there for hours. In the end we asked everyone to make a choice: New Zealand or the UK, with the caveat that we would reassess either choice after six, eighteen and twenty-four months. The UK was the unanimous decision.'

You know your kids, and you may know how they're going to react to the news, so if you see anger, tears and fear coming, be prepared with tissues and chocolate, and remember there could be some door slamming and shouting if it's not what they want.

It could be that your child isn't old enough to understand what's really going on, or you might have a teen who'll be broken-hearted at leaving her first boyfriend behind and she is never, ever, going to forgive you for this. On the flip side, if your son hates his school and has been bullied, it may be the reprieve he's been looking for and the new start he has been wishing for, making you his hero.

Joanna March says, 'I told my son we were moving home so he could live close to his gran and go to school with people who were less likely to move away. It was tough as he was born in Thailand so is a "third culture kid (TCK)". My home and my normal wasn't his, but I think it was easier because he was much younger. He is still (at age thirteen) close to friends he made in Reception, which makes me feel really happy.'

As much as you might be dreading telling your kids about your plans, once the news is out, you've taken away an element of fear. Dealing with the unknown can take up more headspace than the actual reality of their reaction, so do think about this.

Be Honest about Why You're Relocating

You know the reason for this move, but your twelve- and fifteen-year-olds might need some convincing on the motivation behind packing up a life they think is pretty perfect, and will resent leaving their friends and having to start over at a new school, alone.

You need to be honest and clear about why you're going. Try to keep calm and think about it from their point of view. Adjust your language so they can see what's in it for them. Here are some ideas and examples for how you could approach this:

- We're moving to America for Mum's amazing promotion, which means you'll get to go to a really cool school, and we can go and watch the Chicago Bulls at the weekend.
- Going back to Yorkshire means you'll be closer to your cousins, and, even better, they can't wait for you to go to their swimming club and Scouts with them.

- Being in London means you'll have access to all the museums and galleries you love, as well as being able to go to a school that specialises in art.
- We know you really enjoy cycling, so being close to a forest means you can go off-road, rather than dealing with all the buses and traffic in Nottingham.
- Cyprus is the next place for our military adventure, and with this base there is a huge swimming pool. Some of your old friends are already there and waiting for you to arrive.

If the reasons for moving aren't totally positive and you don't really want to be going anywhere new – maybe you're going through a divorce, have lost your business or have to go back to your ailing parents – if you can find a silver lining, please do. We're the adults in all of this, so try not to let your anger, disappointment and frustration eat into their perception of the move. Try to find the support you need to deal with this.

I know these conversations can be hard, so talk it over with your partner or a family member, and if you need to write notes before you talk to your children go for it. I know the pressure is on and you want to make this as painless for them as possible, even if their hearts are breaking. You've totally got this.

Get Them Involved

Even as you wait for the ice to thaw and the tears to stop, you can start to make this exciting and part of that will be with you and the new home you're moving to.

One of my favourite hobbies is looking at Rightmove. While you might have decided on the location and even put an offer in on a house, you could let your child do a bit of house-hunting online once you have told them where you're going. Talk about what they love about your home at the moment, the things that are important to them in a new house (broadband could be a non-negotiable here) and what their dream home would look like – this can be exciting, but you may have to start buying lottery tickets if they are after a home gym and a pool.

Bringing some fun and excitement into the move – even if you're being treated like the bad guy – could help to diffuse animosity and bring out the promise of moving somewhere totally different. Maybe where you're moving is close to a massive park, the beach or even an outstanding BMX track, which could help get their attention and lead them to your way of thinking.

Once you have found a house, or if you're at the stage of visiting (see Chapter Four), take them with you, let them see the property, maybe let them choose their room, explore the garden and even look at where you could set up their Xbox or keep their bikes. All this can help make it feel more inviting and as though they really are being considered.

When we moved to Devon, my sons were of course excited about being by the sea, but one of the deal-clinchers for us was that the house we rented came with a hot tub, and that made them very happy!

Whether it's choosing the colour scheme for their new bedroom, reading the prospectus for their new school or selling old books and toys to get the cash together for a new bike, getting your children involved in your move and letting them be a part of the decision-making process can add a positive dimension into their lives, which could feel anything but normal now.

Give Them a Timeline

'Moving day is tomorrow' will have little impact on a two-year-old other than gathering up her toys in a backpack and shoving crisps in her pockets for the drive. However, this could be a step too far for older children who need to be mentally prepared for the changes that are coming.

I know not everyone who relocates has the luxury of time, and if you're moving for work or with the military, you could be dancing to the beat of someone else's drum, not at a pace that is conducive to packing up teenage dreams. However, the longer they have to pack up – on all levels – the better. This again comes down to honesty, and letting them know what you think will be happening and when. For many there's the consideration of schooling and if you can plan to move during the holidays – the summer holidays, preferably – that can make leaving one place and starting somewhere new just a little bit easier.

Once you have a definite date for moving, let them know, add details into calendars and talk about it because it's those honest, open lines of communication that will make things easier and more likely that starting over will be a success, even if not overnight.

Let Them Talk It Out

Once you've told them you're going, let them know your door is always open to talk about what's going on and how they're feeling. The last thing they might want to do is talk to you, but knowing they can ask questions and be heard, without fear of being told off, is important. The more honest you are with them about why you're moving, the easier it will be to tackle their fears.

Just as you might be feeling anxious about the move, worrying about how your new job will work out and how easy it might be to make friends, your children will be in exactly the same boat and could have 101 questions buzzing around their head. While you don't want to force them to talk through their fears, be sure they know you're there for them, even in the middle of the night, to discuss the worries they have, the angst they feel about being separated from their bestie, and the belief that Ella is totally going to steal their boyfriend even before the removal lorry pulls out of your drive – true story.

Making new friends is likely to be a key concern for your children, especially if you have teenagers. So, as they shout and cry, kick walls and swear, remember they'll be feeling a lot of fear about what's ahead. If you let them feel their feelings now (within reason), your relocation could be a success and resentment-free (well, most of the time) in the longer term.

Make It Fun

One thing to try to keep in mind is that while slicing your fingers on packing boxes and chasing your solicitor on the unusual boundaries at your new house doesn't feel like fun, if you can add this into the mix for your children, it will help. If this is seen as an exciting adventure that they're part of (when they're younger this might be easier), rather than an arduous task they resent or something that is scary and could be a disaster, it makes it so much easier to navigate.

Cecile Blaireau, an ex-teacher, mum and parenting blogger at The Frenchie Mummy, says, 'Don't fear change. Relocating can be scary, but every challenge is a great opportunity to learn, for both parents and children. Plus, an adventure is always exciting. It will help create a stronger bond with your children. And remember that kids are super resilient. Parents naturally want to protect them, but they usually adapt well to new settings.'

Jo Henderson adds, 'We tried to always keep it positive and fun. It helped that we were moving to the sunshine, that the beach was down the road, that Disneyland wasn't far away and that we had a pool in our backyard. It was quite an easy sell!'

Plan sleepovers with friends for your kids before you leave, visit all the places you love while you're still in your current home, and even help them to pack their things, and take the belongings they don't want to the charity shop – these are all things we did in the run-up to our relocation to Devon. A surprise trip to Disneyland Paris also helped to soften the blow!

Talk about Education

When I was researching this book, one of the most common topics people talked about was schooling and relocating, and that was no surprise. When I was a child, you went to the local school and that was that; today, life with kids seems to be governed by league charts, SATs results, whether you live in a grammar-school area, and those all-important Ofsted reports. These will be concerns that you carry with you when you move.

At the end of the day, if you're relocating with kids, they'll have to go to a new school, but the most important thing is that they are happy in the right place for them. From my own experiences of moving to get into a school because of the glowing Ofsted reports, it doesn't always work out, and you need to do what is best for your child, not what might look good on paper.

When we relocated to Devon, my sons were seven and nine. I think it was a pretty good age to make the transition and we had the luxury of being able to determine our own timeframe, something I know not everyone has. However, their happiness and well-being was our priority, so we started with our school search before we even looked for somewhere to live.

The fact that my son has gone through multiple orthopaedic operations meant we had specific requirements for him and his brother, which led us to an independent school, but we looked at all of the options, and started our search about a year before we even decided that Devon was going to be where we settled. What we did know, however, was that starting somewhere midterm would be tough, so we geared everything around being able to get to the coast in the summer holidays, for a September start – and that's what we did. Not only was it a good idea to join at the start of the new academic year when everyone was fresh from the break, but we had a great summer getting to know somewhere new, somewhere we now call home.

Simon Lockyer, Headmaster at Royal Hospital School, often speaks to prospective parents about relocating, and says, 'If possible, try to time your move during the summer holidays so that your son or daughter can have a bit of time to settle in at home, and they can start a new school year rather than part of the way through. Make sure they can attend any induction days ahead of the start of term as this will help to alleviate any new school worries come September. At Royal Hospital School we have thorough induction days before the start of the new school year for new pupils, which is a brilliant opportunity to make friends ahead of starting school. We run fun and informal team-building and orientation exercises for two days, and they meet their house staff so that day one is less daunting.'

We wondered if our children would drift away from some of their friends as moving day approached, and start to feel apprehensive about starting over somewhere new and making friends with kids who have known each other for ever, but by being upfront and honest with them, as well as going to trial days at their new school, we navigated the challenge well. In fact, it was me who let the side down in the end, by crying at the school gates on that last day.

The reality is there is no ideal time to change schools, and Lucy Davies agrees with this: 'We're trying to decide if we should relocate at least a year before our (slightly sensitive) eldest moves up to high school – so that she has time to get used to things and make friends in a smaller primary school environment. Or whether moving her just before Year 7 would be okay since all the kids have the same upheaval when they change schools. The jury is still out – but I'm inclined to try for no later than Year 6 (she's in Year 3 now) so that she has friends to start high school with.'

There are so many things to consider, and it can feel overwhelming, even putting people off making the move at all, but it's worth putting in the time and effort to get it right.

What to Look for in a New School

What you look for in a good school for your child is going to be different from anyone else. While there are going to be the standard needs of good pastoral care, academic results, class sizes and diversity, it's the finer points that make this such a personal choice and one that could divide you and your partner, or wider family members.

A great art department, SEN provision, outstanding sporting facilities, afterschool clubs, a good number of teaching assistants and a well-stocked library are just some of the criteria people look for. If they are important to you and your child, don't disregard them because this could impact the success of your relocation.

Simon Lockyer says, 'Look out for a school with a broad offering – not only so that your child's current interests are covered but also so that they can try new things. Sometimes they can surprise you (and themselves) with the activities they enjoy. From fencing and debating to horse-riding and sailing, Royal Hospital School has more than 200 afterschool clubs to choose from. Group activities and sports are an excellent way for your child to meet and make new friends, improve their confidence and support physical and mental well-being – all of which will prove invaluable in helping them settle into their new location.'

Siân Smith teaches English in Romania, and adds, 'Do your research about the area that you're relocating to and the diversity of schools in that area. Think about public and private schools, state schools, grammar schools, international schools, schools for children with additional needs as well as gender-specific and mixed-gender schools, as this will allow you to make an informed decision about the education of your child and ensure you're making the correct choice for their personality type, aptitudes and abilities. If this move is within the UK, you should also read the most recent school Ofsted report to gauge an understanding of the school's strengths and weaknesses, to make an informed decision.'

Cecile Blaireau agrees with looking at Ofsted reports but doesn't think it's the most important detail and says, 'When I looked for a school for my son to start at Reception I looked at how they stretched more able students and supported the less able, as well as what resources they had for the SEN department. Did they offer languages and, if so, which ones and how often were they taught? I wanted to know if there were any afterschool clubs, and did they put an emphasis on learning through play? Did they have good artistic and PE resources? Were the children stimulated with individual and group work? Was there diverse learning?'

Visiting schools, talking to the head, having a tour, looking at classrooms and getting a feel for how happy the students seem to be are great ways to get a feel for somewhere that's an intrinsic part of your child's life. I know my son's school has been key to the success of our move to Devon, and while it's years before they leave, I already feel sad in anticipation of that day.

You can look on websites for the details of open days, or call them directly to set up an appointment. This is also a good time to find out about the application process. There will be areas where good schools are totally oversubscribed and having proof of address is needed before you get on to a waiting list, but also be wary of a school with many free places, and ask why that is the case.

Remember, you aren't going to the school, your child is. The older they are, the more vital it is that they get a say in where they will go to school and have some input into the decision-making process.

Simon Lockyer agrees, and says, 'It's a good idea to make your child part of the research and moving process – take them to visit schools and listen to their thoughts on which one they like the most. Make a list, together, of questions to ask all the schools you're considering when you visit so that you can compare them equally. You can also request to meet some pupils and the headmaster on school tours to help you both get a real feel for the place. At Royal Hospital School, we will also introduce you to existing parents at the school in your child's year group to help you settle in, so it's worth asking prospective schools if they offer this too.'

Research, visit, research, visit and research again is my advice. Also, be aware that catchment boundaries can change from one year to another, so double check the details before you decide on a new home.

One further point, from my experience, is while you aren't going to the school, you may want to check out the parents. Do they say hello at the gates, is there a kind vibe when they are around? Is there a PTA? Our first school was less than friendly; the cliques were real, and it was a miserable experience I wish I hadn't had to go through.

We do, however, live and learn, and the boys now go to a great school with a fantastic community feel because I listened to my gut feeling. You might want to do the same.

What If You're Moving out of the Country?

For some people, relocating means going to a new country, which in turn means entering a new education system. While this can be daunting, the exciting flip side could be not having to wear a uniform, taking a classic yellow bus to high school, and being the cool kid in the class with an unusual accent.

Francesca Aaen's sons moved to a school in Andorra, and she says, 'They were fully brought into the move, but even still the first few months at school were quite a challenge as they got to grips with the languages. We pretty much didn't do any extracurricular clubs for the first year – except an in-school tennis club – so that they could just decompress in the evenings.'

Siân Smith says: 'Do your research into whether the international school is a not-for-profit school or a chain of schools belonging to a private business enterprise. This may provide a hint as to how the school is run and what their main priorities are, including whether money is ploughed back into the school resources or not. I would say, if it is a fee-paying school, compare parental opinions with other international schools in the area. Some parents have sent their children to more than one school and can provide you with the advantages and disadvantages of both. Being an international school, it is also important for parents to thoroughly check which exam specifications and curriculums are being followed. This can impact students' choices later (for example at university level). Some international schools follow the English curriculum, for example, whilst others follow the American curriculum. Some offer A levels in Year 12 and others follow the International Baccalaureate.'

She adds, 'If the schools you're looking at are abroad, there are websites that include testimonials and ratings for that school. Equally, school websites usually provide a solid overview of the ethos of the school, the goals, aims and mission of that school, and you can usually gain a feel for the level of student, parent and community involvement in the school, and how cohesive and collaborative it is. Likewise, check the success rates of any potential school on their website.'

Relocation exercise

Whether you visit one, two or ten schools, the table below will help you keep a record of your thoughts for each, and hopefully make it easier for you to decide which one makes the grade.

	SCHOOL 1	SCHOOL 2	SCHOOL 3
How close is it to our home?			
Is there a bus or can we walk or drive there?			
How many children are there in a class?			
Are there classroom assistants?			
Are there before- and afterschool clubs?			
What are the extracurricular activities like?			
What is the head like?			
Is there a PTA?			
What is the policy on bullying?			
What are the exam results like?			
Did it seem like a happy place?			
What outside space is there?			
Do they offer lunchtime meals?			
Did you like it?			
Did your child like it?			
Notes			

At the end of the day, you're the parents and you'll have your own thoughts, preferences and reservations about each school you go to, but talk to your children about this, listen to what they think, and if they tried a taster day, really discuss how they felt and whether they want to go there. Even the little ones will have an idea of what they think. It could come down to a fun forest school and kind teachers, but if they're having doubts and red flags are there when it comes to any hint of bullying, oversubscribed classes or a lack of ethnic diversity, pay attention so you can get it right the first time.

Once you have decided on the school you want to go for, you'll need to contact them, as well as the necessary authorities, to get the ball rolling and a place, hopefully, allocated.

Good luck!

Be Honest and Don't Overpromise

As guilt rears its ugly head, you might want to tell them it's going to be okay, they'll absolutely make best friends on day one, and, yes, you will totally get a sausage dog when you arrive. However, unless you can 100 per cent guarantee this, don't say it, however much those panda eyes are breaking your heart.

I know it's tempting to give in as they sob and tell you how much they're going to miss Granny, but they'll trust you more if you're honest with them. Be kind, be upfront, but don't make promises you can't keep, or you'll face real problems when your new landlord says no pets.

Karen Marshall makes a good point when she says, 'Think through what you're going to say and what the outcomes could be. We said we would go on a two-year adventure, but in hindsight we should have said that we might come back in a couple of years, but we might stay for longer. At the time we didn't know ourselves, but we didn't talk to them about it in those terms as they were little, so they just hung on to the idea we would go back if they felt they wanted to. And they obviously don't factor in much except themselves.'

Saying Goodbye

Just like you need to say goodbye to those you care about, so do your children, and this won't be easy. Depending on their age, friendship groups and links with the local community, the amount of distress and time this will take will differ, which is why you need to give as much time as you can so they can deal with this. A picnic on the last day of school, a BBQ at your home, or a few meet-ups and sleepovers are all ways that this can be done, so talk to them about what will work for them, and get some dates in the diary.

I would bet money on some tears and tantrums when it comes to saying goodbye, but this is normal and you really can't blame them, so give them time to go through this process.

Now that we all have mobile phones and access to social media, as well as planes, trains and automobiles, this isn't the end; I know my boys speak to friends from our old life online and we see them when we go back. It's not the same as getting the bus to school together or going into town at the weekend, but it's easier than ever to stay in touch and, who knows, they may end up at the same uni one day or working together at NASA! While this might feel like the end of the world right now, these goodbyes aren't the end of a friendship, just the start of a new chapter together.

Remember, in most cases, this relocation is going to be your decision not your children's, so ultimatums and laying down the law might not be the best way to get them onside. What we are doing in this book is making the overall process of relocating successful, so if you do hit a brick wall at this point – maybe they refuse to speak to you, or pack a bag and go and sleep over with their bestie – remember, it won't always be like this. Putting the groundwork in at this time will, hopefully, allow you all to reap relocation rewards in the long run.

Relocation exercise

If your kids are up for it, get them a relocation journal, or have them collect photos before they go to create pictures for their new house. They could hand out cards on their last day at school to their friends with contact details for staying in touch.

Chapter Nine

We Can Work It Out

Work is such a chicken-and-egg situation when it comes to relocating.

Do you find a new job first and then relocate, or do you decide where you truly want to live and look for employment that will make that dream a reality?

The truth is, you don't need to win the lottery or have a fancy trust fund if you want to successfully start over, but you do need to have a plan, a strong work ethic, and the ability to filter out the noise that says you can't do this, because you absolutely can.

Getting your work situation right is an integral part of the relocation puzzle and the fear of getting it wrong is a big reason why people carry on living a life that doesn't fulfil them, or leaves them trawling property sites night after night.

Had I written this book minus a global pandemic, I'm pretty sure this chapter would be very different, because, while COVID had many negative impacts, it opened up the conversation around remote and hybrid working options. I'm not saying that every job can be done from home, but video calls and remote meetings mean the dynamics have changed and there are opportunities out there for the taking.

Tony Gibson, Founder of Clearooms, a workspace management tool, says: 'According to a report by Microsoft, over 70 per cent of employees want flexible remote working options to continue and 65 per cent want the chance to be able to meet their colleagues in person – those aren't two contrary positions; they want the ability to do both. But if that data tells us anything, it's that remote or hybrid working is going to be a deciding factor in whether or not your employees stay or cut and run for somewhere else. Whilst it's true that hybrid and remote working brings benefits in the form of better work–life balance and increased productivity, the larger benefit comes in the form of attracting and retaining staff. Businesses embracing remote working means employees are not tied to a specific location, giving them the freedom to move further afield since they don't need to commute. For example, employees working in Manchester are beginning to rent or purchase property in areas like Warrington.

'This benefit also translates to employers. Not only does this working model allow you to retain staff even if they're moving away from your area, but you're also presented with the opportunity of attracting new staff from far and wide. Now, instead of being forced into recruiting staff within a certain radius, you're able to recruit nationally, allowing you to find the best and brightest of talent regardless of their location.

'Flexible working arguably has the power to make or break employee and employer loyalty. 41 per cent of employees have argued that they would be likely to resign if they were forced to return to the office against their will after working remotely. It's no longer a viable option to simply return to the way things were before. Businesses like Ford, Dropbox, Salesforce, Facebook, Microsoft and Google have already implemented working models like this, showing that tech companies always seem to be ahead of the curve for this stuff. The question is, how long will it take more "traditional" businesses to get with the programme and realise that their workforce is calling out for flexibility?'

My husband and I are both self-employed, so we could move with our work. Starting somewhere new was still a gamble, but one we thought was worth taking. We worked hard and it has been a success, but it wasn't easy, and it did cause heartache and stress at times. I'm sure you'll have your own set of complexities to unpick to make things work for you, but if you're determined enough to make it a success, it will be.

Start Networking Today

Who you know, as well as what you know, can be invaluable when it comes to finding a new job or starting a business venture when you relocate. I'm not talking about outdated old boys' clubs or secret handshakes, but your family, friends, colleagues (past and present), peers and even old bosses may know of opportunities, could have helpful advice and might be happy to give you a glowing testimonial.

Announcing 'I'M MOVING' might not be possible now, but if relocating is on the cards, start networking today. This doesn't mean you're sneaking around or being deceitful, but you're planning ahead, so the smart money is building your network. Facebook friends, Instagram buddies, LinkedIn connections and Twitter peeps are there as potential aides, so call on them to help you successfully start over. Everyone you know, everyone they know, and everyone *they* know could potentially help you find a new job, even if it's a temp role to start with, so don't be shy at asking for help.

Since we moved to Devon, and with the impact of COVID, the ability to network not only locally, but on national and international levels, has grown massively. Joanne Dewberry, aka Networking Ninja, agrees, and says: 'The easiest way to start networking is online. Search for your relocation destination, join Facebook groups; not just one, but a few, try them on for size. Each group will feel and offer something different, so you need to find the ones that best fit you. Twitter has a "hashtag hour" for *everything*, my local hour is #DorsetHour, and you will find a plethora of people willing to help and advise you. Find local publications; most will allow you to subscribe online or have a social media presence. Start interacting with people in all areas of your life – work, social, school, make friends with your new neighbours – they will know the ins and outs of everything.'

While we can do a lot online, going to coffee mornings and evening events will get your face known and allow people to see your enthusiasm. You aren't there yet, but if you're visiting the place you want to move to, and if there's an event taking place at the time, be brave, go along and see what it's all about. Eventbrite is a great place to find out this kind of information as well as social media groups. If you're moving from Manchester to Madrid, being able to hop on a flight to attend networking events could be extremely difficult, but the power of the internet means you can do the groundwork remotely. If something comes up that could be good, look at the pros and cons of going and if it's too good to miss, tie it in with another trip.

Relocating with Your Current Employer

Moving because of your job, or your partner's, can be a once-in-a-lifetime opportunity, but that doesn't mean there aren't pros and cons to weigh up, as well as questions to ask and decisions to make.

Going from Middlesbrough to Madrid or Newcastle to Nevada sounds amazing on paper, but as with all relocations, you will need to make sure everyone involved is in agreement (maybe not your one-year-old, though the move could upset grandparents) before you sign on the dotted line.

Leah Eser has relocated with her employer twice and says, 'My advice for someone who's moving with their current employer is to make sure you thoroughly review your relocation package and, if need be, negotiate. My inexperience meant that my relocation package was definitely not great, my salary was much lower than the market standards and I only got one return ticket home. Once I arrived and talked to others who had relocated with the company, they had relocated with a higher salary as well as annual return tickets home.'

You may already be in talks with your organisation, or it could be you that's pushing for the move abroad. Whichever it is, get the foundations in place from the get-go. Using the questions below could be a solid starting point:

- Is the new job something you'll enjoy, and will it progress your career?
- Is there a relocation package and will your company help with finding somewhere new to live and schools for your children?
- Does the salary you're being offered reflect the cost of living somewhere new? For example, when I was a teacher in Tokyo

I had a great salary, but it was £5 for a loaf of bread, and you wouldn't get much change from £20 when ordering a G&T in a Ginza bar.

- Will your partner be able to get a new job in the location you're moving to?
- Is there a vibrant, inclusive expat community and how easy would it be to fit into local life?
- What local laws and religions will impact the lifestyle and freedom you and your family will have?
- How long will your commute be?
- Will you be able to have flexible working?
- How will this impact your family? Consider the good and bad.
- Can family and friends visit?
- What happens if you don't take the package?
- Is this right for you?

As with all things relocation, do your research and make the right choice for you. That could mean some serious soul-searching and asking yourself difficult questions, but this is about successfully starting over, so you need to get it right, however uncomfortable it might feel.

Securing a New Job before You Move

You've decided that London, with its bars, shops, galleries and restaurants, has been fun, but you want a house with a garden as your kids grow up. That somewhere could be closer to your parents. While it won't offer the same theatre options and endless exhibitions, it's practical for the future, means you can spend days on the beach, as well as having places at good schools.

That's all great as a plan on paper, but if you need a bigger mortgage, you might not be able to pack up and ship out straight away. You could start planning your next career move with these factors in mind. If you know your current employer can't offer flexible or remote working and there isn't an office or location closer to your new home town, you'll have to do some planning.

Steps you can take are:

- Update your CV to include all your current duties, experience, skills and abilities. This is not the time to be coy if you want a job that will help you secure the beautiful garden you've always wanted.
- Speak to head-hunters and recruiters to see what the landscape is like and whether they can suggest businesses and other recruiters in the area you want to move to, so you can speak to them.
- Sign up to job alerts – but I wouldn't suggest using your work email address for this as you never know who might see the opportunities that are coming in!
- Read trade press; for example, I'm always looking at *PR Week* for new opportunities.
- Let your network know you're looking to make a change, but be aware of who you tell at this point. Word spreads fast and you don't want difficult conversations with your manager if you aren't ready for that.
- Double check your contract, just so you know the terms and conditions of your current job. Look for your notice period, rules on moving to a competitor and using up any holiday before you go (those days could be time off to visit somewhere new or go to interviews, so be sharp with this).
- Take advantage of any training you can get. If that means extra work in your spare time to do a course in leadership or a social media diploma, do it!

If you're really lucky, and the stars are aligned, the perfect job in your dream location could come along, and you could be in your new place in time for Christmas. However, it's not always that smooth, so actively looking for new roles, being proactive in your approach, and setting yourself up for change will help your relocation be a success when it does happen.

While there are jobs that don't offer the option to work from home, many do, and that means the relocation dream is more possible than ever. For many, being chained to a desk from 9 a.m. to 6 p.m. isn't necessarily a prerequisite for keeping your job.

Finding a New Job When You Arrive

Yes, you can move without having a job lined up, but my suggestion – and it's a strong one at that – is to start your search before arriving at your destination, not afterwards. If you aren't going to have a job from day one of starting over, having savings in place as a buffer is a plan worth considering. Being able to cover your expenses for at least three months, if not six, could take the pressure off you. If you find something sooner, great; if not, with this pot in place, it's not the end of the world and won't scupper your plans to start over altogether.

If this is the way you're going to do it, ensure you have an up-to-date CV ready to go when you do start to look around.

You can mention the move in your personal statement, which would help explain short gaps in your employment history. In that time you could have learnt valuable skills such as budgeting, house-selling (if you sold a property yourself), as well as marketing, photography or learning a new language as a result of this massive life change, so add these in.

If you don't have your heart set on working for a particular company, find out who the major employers in town are by doing a quick Google search and do your homework on them. Look at companies that are featured in the local newspapers and websites, search out what companies are growing to get a sense of the economic landscape, and keep an eye on their social media accounts.

If you're hoping to move to a seaside town, like St Ives, for example, a lot of the local work will be centred around tourism and the hospitality industry, so go back to why you are moving, as well as your skill set. If the types of jobs available aren't in alignment, it might not work for you. It could be, however, that you and your partner are teachers, and you find out that Cornwall is calling out for education staff, so it would be perfect. The opportunities are certainly out there, you just need to do your research, network, and find what is going to be workable, and successful, for you.

Relocation exercise

Create a list of ten companies in your preferred region you'd like to work for and do your homework on each. Read their websites, find out the details of their HR department, look at current opportunities, follow them on social media – LinkedIn is a great place to start – and then make sure your CV is up to date so you can start making contact.

If you really want this relocation to work, now is not the time to be shy; it's the time to be brave, proactive and to go for what you want, because if you don't someone else will.

Part-time Work to Tide You Over

You might want to find a full-time job, but-part time work could be your ticket to freedom.

Don't rule out applying for temporary and part-time jobs, especially in situations where you really want to move, perhaps because you want to get your kids into a new school for the new term, or you need to be closer to your parents as they require extra support.

Stepping in as a barista at a beachside coffee shop might not stretch your bookkeeping skills, but it could be a fantastic way to meet new people, get discounts on food and drinks, and when the owners find out more about you, they may well ask you to help out with their accounts. Stacking shelves, doing admin, cleaning or taking on delivery work are all ways of keeping the cash coming in. While they might not be your dream job, they'll help make your dream relocation a success – which is what we want.

Don't think of this as taking a step backwards, but rather an indication of your dedication to doing something you 100 per cent believe in. Remember, future employers will be impressed by your willingness to apply yourself, to get stuck in, and your resilience and tenacity could be skills they need for their business.

Retraining

If you've wanted to change your work and do something new, relocating could give you the chance to do that. Maybe you want to move out of marketing and become a primary school teacher, or you might hate your office job and being in a city could give you the chance to do work experience at a newspaper and retrain as a journalist on the job.

If you're moving because of a job change for your partner, this could allow you to follow your dreams, which is really exciting and an example of relocation silver linings.

Do your research, find out about courses in the area you're moving to, look at online learning, talk to a career coach, and really work out what you want to do next.

Setting Up on Your Own

Relocating can be the turning point you need to finally start your own business, or it could be the reason behind your move. Being a business owner isn't for the faint-hearted; it takes grit, determination and hard graft, just like relocating. With so many people dreaming to be their own boss, this could be your time to shine.

Maybe you want to set up a photography business in Arizona, you've always dreamt of running a pub in Lancashire, or having a graphic design studio by the water in Norfolk has been calling you for years. Well, a relocation could make all of this possible.

At this point, I would suggest you:

- Write a business plan and get serious about making this work.
- Do your number crunching and get your finance in place, costing in everything from desks and computers to staff, electricity, insurance, business tax and branding.
- Speak to a financial adviser or your bank manager about your options and make sure you have a robust plan in place.
- Do as much reading, listening, networking and learning as you can.

- If you're going to be working from home, or even a local site, do check the Wi-Fi and phone services. You might want to run a B&B in the Isle of Skye, but if people can't get on to your website to book a holiday and you can't run your social media, you will need to rethink your tech set-up.

If you are starting your own business, you'll want to have money in the bank to help if things take longer to get off the ground than expected, and in order to cover unexpected costs. It could also be that you need to continue with the day job for a while until you're up and running and ready to make the move 100 per cent. You could take on a part-time job to tide you over until you're ready to launch.

Taking a Career Break

For some people, a relocation comes with a career break. Maybe your husband or wife is starting a new job and you want to be at home for a while, getting things sorted out, settling the kids at school, and unpacking your furniture and belongings. At the heart of this book isn't judgement about how you achieve your relocation; it's about doing what's right for you.

Don't underestimate what goes into relocating, on an emotional, financial, physical and mental level. If you can take some time out from your work to make it a success, it could be the best decision you make of all.

I love the book *The Squiggly Career* by Helen Tupper and Sarah Ellis because it looks at how you can create work that is right for you, and this could help if you're wondering just how to make this fit for a successful relocation.

If It's Not Just You

What if it's not just you who needs to consider work when you move? Maybe it's your job that's behind this relocation, or you're packing up and shipping out because your husband has been promoted, or your daughter has set up a hotel near Loch Ness.

You need to consider the work situation of everyone who's part of your move, if you want your relocation to be a success.

Relocation exercise

You don't want to get overwhelmed with alerts and reminders, but start thinking about the types of networking that could work for you. Join a few groups, look at Twitter, sign up for Eventbrite, and check out the lie of the land to see what opportunities and connections there are out there.

Chapter Ten

Don't Let Stress Take Over

Spoiler alert: relocation is exciting, but it can be extremely stressful, even if you're moving to your forever home in your dream location.

Feeling overwhelmed during the process is normal, so rather than seeing these emotions as a signal to stop your plans, view them as a sign that you need to slow down and look after yourself if you want to make a success of the transition.

From telling family and friends to handing in your notice, dealing with the disappointment of delayed mortgage offers and broken mugs on moving day, this is not going to be plain sailing. But there are ways that you can manage rising anxiety, so it doesn't take over and totally ruin the experience.

I would be amazed if your move went without at least one hitch, even a small one, that sent your pulse racing and caused doubts to creep in, but just as you take care of these issues, it's paramount that you take care of yourself. You might think that this is a luxury you can ill afford, but I would argue with that and say it is a necessity you can't live without.

While a weekend at a spa mid-move probably won't be on the cards, there are some simple things you can do to look after yourself when the packing boxes are stacked against you and it all feels a bit too much.

You might be tired, worried about the kids missing their friends, and sick and tired of lugging bin liners to the dump and charity shop, which means being kind to yourself and those around you is vital.

I'm pretty sure there will be a few cross words and tense encounters along the way, but this doesn't make you a bad person, or your relocation a mistake. It's the move – not you!

I know I'm being really obvious, but what is it that makes moving so stressful? Well, it's not that just one thing is changing – it's EVERYTHING!

The location you live in, the home you live in, the layout of your home, the loss of friends, a change of job ... Even if it's the move of a lifetime to the sunny beaches of Santa Monica, your life is in flux and often in the hands of so many people and factors that are out of your control.

I know that when the removal company double-books, the kids don't want to go to a new school and the dog wees on the floor, a smile might not be on your face, but if we lose sight of the prize, our ability to look after ourselves falls faster than your blood sugar after scoffing another Mars Bars washed down with an energy drink. Remember why you're doing this, and it will make wiping up that mess and booking a self-drive van just a bit easier.

If you're feeling more tired and anxious than normal, it's key to look after yourself the same way you're caring for others and keeping their relocation needs met. However excited or anxious you are about your new life, there's a lot of extra work involved, and the upheaval and uncertainty will take a toll on you, even at a subconscious level, and with sleep even more scarce than normal, it's so important that you're kind to yourself.

Suzanne Betlem, a physical trainer, knows all about this and says: 'When you're stressed out, under pressure, overworked and overwhelmed, taking good care of yourself feels like something you simply do not have the time or energy for. The more you need self-care, the less you're likely to invest in it. It is as true as it is diabolically ironic.

'Moving house can supercharge you and boost your energy, but it is also very stressful. Changes, for most people, are naturally stressful. They take you out of your routine, mess with your set ways and structures and can leave you feeling shaken. Self-care is the key to getting you through these unsettling times. But how? First you have to understand that self-care is not a luxury, it is a *necessity*. You remember the flight attendant's instruction of putting on your own oxygen mask before helping others? Well, taking care of yourself is like putting on an oxygen mask; you need it in order to survive.'

Take Some Exercise

Going for a run, taking a spin class or sweating it out at Zumba will help you feel energised, and centred, and there's nothing like a shot of feel-good endorphins to boost your mood and clear your mind.

Yes, you might need to cancel your gym membership before you move, but it could be that you can pay as you go for classes. If you enjoy running, your running mates will be there until the very last day. Keeping up your exercise is only going to help during your move, even if you need to modify it a little.

Suzanne Betlem knows that exercising is a great distraction from the overwhelming instabilities that come with relocating, as well as a fantastic way to keep fit. She says: 'Relocating is super exciting, and it is exhilarating to take such a big step, but it can turn your world upside down, so adding exercise to your schedule clears your head and releases tension in your body. So, make use of it! Don't regard exercise as an additional burden, but instead embrace it as your new coping mechanism. In practical terms, I would suggest implementing an exercise routine well ahead of your relocation. Keep it simple and familiarise yourself with it so that when the sh*t hits the fan, it is something you can fall back on. Choose something that will help you through the transitional period. Your (new) workout routine should be something that is enjoyable, accessible and doesn't require an extensive range of materials.

'Something as simple as rope skipping or going for a run two or three times a week might just do the trick for you. If you're into resistance or strength training, you could use resistance bands or a kettlebell. Or try a bodyweight workout. A personal trainer can help you set up your new fitness habit, but make sure they understand you need something sweet and simple to get you through the hectic transitional phase. Once you're set up in your new location, you can start something more elaborate, join a gym or a sports club of your choice, which is also a great way to make friends and feel a part of something, somewhere new.'

Since moving time is so busy, if you can, prioritise your exercise time as the first thing you do in the morning, as this can help avoid the temptation of postponing it when you start to wane. This can also be a great way to ensure you start your day feeling revitalised, centred and accomplished.

Eat Well

I know, I know, you're busy and it's easier to order a pizza or grab a burger when there's so much to do, but filling up on fast food and takeaways won't give you the energy you need for moving. There may be evenings when you phone out for food because you're too tired to move another muscle, and that's fine, but for the majority of the time ensure you're eating a well-balanced diet full of fresh fruit and veg, good proteins and fats. Keep healthy snacks in reach, and don't forget to drink lots of water.

Drinking endless cups of tea and coffee, as well as glugging energy drinks, might give you a quick hit of caffeine but it's a sure way to hit the wall later and end up feeling groggy, dehydrated and lacking the energy to do the jobs in hand. It's all about moderation, but fuel your body and mind well, and they'll thank you.

Anna Thomson, a nutritionist and Founder and Director of Nourishing Families CIC, agrees that moving is right up there with the most stressful events you can experience. She says: 'When we experience stress, our nervous system responds by releasing a flood of hormones, including adrenalin and cortisol, which get the body ready for action. Before an important meeting or deadline, a little bit of pressure can be helpful. But the relocation process can drag on for months, leading to ongoing stress.

'Insulin helps maintain blood sugar levels. It also reduces the stress hormone cortisol and increases appetite, so it makes perfect sense that we crave sugar and reach for refined carbs, energy drinks and snacks when under stress. Yet if we rely on these, we're more likely to feel exhausted, wired and anxious. The key is to keep well hydrated and stabilise our blood sugar levels.

'Balanced meals with a mix of protein, complex carbs, lots of vegetables and a little fat will provide sustained energy so that you can focus on what needs to be done. Cut down on the coffee and include antioxidant-rich green tea (though it still is high in caffeine) and herbal teas such as redbush chai. Instead of fizzy or energy drinks, have sparkling water and lemon or a splash of elderflower cordial.

'If you've mostly packed away your kitchen or have limited cooking facilities, it can be hard to eat well so buy pre-prepared meals or foods that need minimal cooking. Here are some examples: pouches of precooked grains, multi-seeded crackers, noodles that just need soaking, marinated tofu or tempeh, boiled eggs, toasted nuts or seeds, frozen prawns or edamame, smoked mackerel, cherry tomatoes, vacuum-packed cooked beetroot, washed salad leaves and prepared vegetables. By eating well, you should feel sustained with better energy levels that enable you to keep going.'

We all know that when we move it can be stressful for you, and your family dynamic can be out of sync, with a tendency to snap at the ones you love and they at you. Mindfulness teacher Judy Claughton suggests that by making time to be present together for food, talking about the move and other things over meals, you can diffuse some of the tension. She says, 'Be mindful as you eat, even if you have to eat on your laps or are grabbing a quick picnic at the park. Avoid the temptation to eat with the TV – this might be the only proper conversation you have all day!'

Get Out in Nature

I find one of the most relaxing, grounding things to do when moving (or at any time, really) is to get out into nature. Whether it's the local park, woods or the beach, being outside in the fresh air, without Wi-Fi and my to-do list, really helps set my mind free.

Pamela Spence, a medical herbalist, agrees with me on this and says, 'My core belief is that tuning in to nature is the quickest, easiest, most profound way to reduce your stress levels. So try to find a green space near you that you can go to – either to walk or just to be – and feel the stress leave your body. This also has the knock-on effect of helping you get to know your new neighbourhood, and that in itself will help your body reduce the alert levels more quickly. If you don't have green space near you, look out of your windows – can you see trees? An area of sky? That'll do. Concentrate on the nature you can see and breathe deeply.'

I know that if you're knee-deep in decluttering and still have 101 things to do, going outside might feel frivolous, but it could help ground you, bring down your stress levels and ease any feelings of panic.

Judy believes we can look for strength from the elements, and says, 'When you connect to earth, air, fire and water – it's a conscious shift that will bring you a sense of power and balance. Step outside and lift up your arms and as you lift them back behind your body, imagine drawing the strength of the sun into your body. Notice the support of the ground beneath your feet. Deepen this by taking off your shoes. Find water and feel its coolness and freshness on your fingers – damp grass, rain drops, a spray of the hose, even just touching a plant near you and holding a hand on your chest and appreciating the water in you and the plant. Lastly, become aware of the air on your skin, breathe deep and allow it to freshen you up and enliven your body and mind.'

Read a Book

There's nothing like getting lost in a book. It can be the relaxing medicine you need when you're mid-move and need to switch off the stress. Reading this book might be helping you feel calmer and more excited about your upcoming relocation, or if you're using your move to start up a new business, there are plenty of books out there to get you on your way, but how about disappearing into the pages of a thriller?

If reading isn't your thing, listening to audiobooks is a brilliant way to tune your brain in to something other than the jobs you need to do to get you relocated.

Oh, and don't forget to take back any library books before you move, and sign up with a new library once you're settled in your new location – not only will it give you access to a whole new catalogue of books, but it could be a good place to make friends and build your new support network.

Slow Down

You might think you don't have time for this, but mediation and yoga could be your best friends when it comes to easing the stress of relocating.

Meditation is a brilliant way to tune out of the craziness of the moving world and just be in the present moment. I find that even fifteen minutes in the morning, before tackling my to-do list, can give me clarity and peace at a time when I most need it, and that includes moving.

Judy Claughton says, 'There's a saying in meditation circles, "Support your well-being by meditating for twenty minutes a day, and when you're too busy, meditate for forty minutes", and, no, I didn't make a typo there. The busier we are, the more we need to care for our well-being. A formal meditation and mindfulness practice can help you switch that focus back so you feel more in control.'

Whether you meditate alone, use an app or join an online session, this can be a brilliant way to focus on you and let the stress of boxes, estate agents and school application forms fade away.

As a yoga teacher, Jacqui Doyle believes this practice can help ease the anxiety and stress of moving house. She says, 'Yoga stimulates the parasympathetic nervous system, and we can counter stress by, amongst other things, slowing the heart rate, relaxing the muscles to release tension, increasing our digestive system, and thus restoring balance to our body. By practising controlled breathing techniques and postures, you will feel calmer, less stressed, or anxious, with improved sleep and thus improved general health and well-being.'

While you might not have the time to get to a class, or maybe you haven't found a new one to join, remember that there are lots of online apps out there – as well as virtual sessions that could work well – so do check out what's available.

Take and Ask for Help

You know the drill: you do it all, get the removal quotes, order the packing boxes, speak to the letting agent, search for new schools, do endless trips to the tip and one day you buckle and shout, 'Can't anyone *help* me?'

Well, they can, but you have to ask them rather than trying to prove you've got this and playing the martyr when it gets too much.

Look at how you can draft in support as you plan your move and call on your network, because I know you'd do the same for them. Yes, there are going to be people who you won't want to ask because you know they don't want you to go, but others will be there to help look after the kids or watch the dog for the weekend while you look at properties in Oxford, or it could simply be your partner doing the food shop so you can complete forms and speak to landlords.

There are no medals for doing it all on your own, but there are rewards for calling in help, and I know which one I'd rather do!

Relocation exercise

Draw up a list of jobs that you don't necessarily have to do yourself, and look at who you can ask to help ease the load to ensure you don't burn out before you even leave your current house. Then, ask people to help!

Get Some Sleep

You might be tempted to burn the candle at both ends when your to-do list is growing by the minute, and it feels like you're never going to close the door to your current home, but there are only so many productive hours in a day. The temptation might be to pack just one more box or clean out one more cupboard before you go to bed, but staying up all night won't help anyone, especially you, so pace yourself.

Give yourself a deadline to stop each day, sit down, watch TV, have a nutritious meal, drink some water, and turn off that relocation button as you soak in the bath or do some gentle stretches to ease your muscles and the tension in your neck and back.

Make sure your bedroom isn't packing-box central; keep it clean and tidy. When you get into bed, don't use that time to make one last list for the day – rest up and you will feel recharged the next day.

Anna Thomson reminds us not to forget about sleep, and says, 'Satchin Panda, the circadian rhythms researcher, states that losing three hours of sleep between 10 p.m. and 5 a.m. amounts to the same effect as shift work leading to a negative impact on health. It may be tempting to keep going with packing or sorting into the small hours, especially if you have kids to sort out. When relocating from Japan back to the UK a few years ago and running out of time, we switched it around. We went to bed early, around 9:30 to 10 p.m. and woke at 4 a.m. to pack before the kids woke up. Admittedly, it was hard to get up but once we got going, we found that we were much more focused, alert and productive than if we had stayed up late.'

Relocation exercise

When you're feeling stressed, get your relocation journal out and write things down. Getting your feelings out of your head and on to paper is really cathartic. It means you don't need to rant on Facebook or shout at your partner because they aren't as stressed out as you – much better to put your thoughts down somewhere safe.

Remember to read back your words once you're settled somewhere new, and you'll see just how far you have come and how much you can do when the pressure is on and you want a successful outcome.

Chapter Eleven

Shutting Down the Doubts

Relocating isn't just a case of moving around the corner, it's a massive life change. Therefore, having doubts is something you may well encounter. Now, those could be your doubts, or those of your partner, mum, cousins, anyone, really; but at the end of the day, this is your life, your choice and your future, so get it right for you.

Some of you will be raring to go and 100 per cent sure that this is the best decision you've ever made, but I am pretty sure that for others there will be moments when you wonder what on earth you're doing and question the rationale behind this.

Remember, you did this work in Chapter Two. If you're in doubt now, why not go back and look over the notes you made to help you get clear on the positive things that may come your way if you keep going. Feeling unsure now and again is natural; it doesn't mean you need to abandon plans – you might just need to reassure yourself that you are on the right track.

Lucy Davies has moved before and is contemplating another move in the next couple of years. She says, 'Doubts are definitely an issue for us. We go back and forth about whether the upheaval is worth it. We spent ages chatting recently and decided that a big driver for us both is simply wanting a change. It would be easier in many ways if we were forced into the move because of a job change.'

Debbie Favell has a different spin on the situation: 'We moved as a family from Hertfordshire to a little city in the Canadian prairies in our forties and the worries and "what ifs" were real. "Are we doing the right thing?" "What if it doesn't work?" "'What if the kids hate it?" "What if ...?"

'We talked a lot about having "review" points at six, eighteen and twenty-four months to make sure we were all happy and thriving, and, if not, we would revisit options. We're big believers in "family discussions". The kids are included, and their viewpoints are important. A year in and we felt like we had a pretty good handle on what life had to offer and the work/home balance was a lot better than in the UK. The kids were happy, they had friends, were confident in themselves and in school. I was the only one struggling to find my place and my tribe outside of the home, but it didn't feel like a big enough issue that I either couldn't cope with it or needed to return to the UK. At eighteen months we had an 1,800-mile move for a work transfer for my husband so that provided another new environment. We have now been in Canada for four years and are awaiting permanent residency.'

Doubts are real and will be different for everyone. They will come and go.

Eve Menezes Cunningham adds, 'I didn't have doubts about it being the right thing to do, but I had no idea how I was going to make it work. On the one hand, I fully expected to wake up with the whim to move home the first few days. Instead, my intention felt stronger.'

Your partner might not be sure if they could cope with the commute, and maybe they don't feel confident about finding something new. You need to talk about this, because if the issues aren't resolved now, you could end with resentment eating into your new life and success could be scuppered when he doesn't find anyone to play golf with after all.

Doubts around the impact on children as they get older is something Naomi Breese McKiernan is only too aware of. She says, 'We've relocated a few times. Each was different. Our initial move took us from home and family. We were excited, but our families were sad. The next time my husband wanted to move, but I didn't and felt it would be tough on our toddler. The last time none of us really wanted to leave and having a junior school-aged child was a real wrench. I think there were always doubts but as the kids get older and the effects of our choices affect them more, my doubts have increased.'

Let's not forget that the doubts of family and friends, as well as colleagues and bosses who simply don't want you to change the status quo of life and how it is today, can totally cloud your judgement.

Other people have definitely tried to sow seeds of doubt in my head when I've gone somewhere new; be that leaving the safety of the suburbs at eighteen, heading to Japan at twenty-two or moving to Devon in my forties. I'm a strong-willed, determined woman and if someone tries to stop me doing something, that makes me even more determined to do it and prove them wrong. I knew what I was doing was the right thing for me and my family, so their words didn't determine my final decision, but I did consider the comments that came my way and addressed them accordingly.

Yes, people can be concerned, but it's not up to anyone else to understand why you're going because, at the end of the day, this is your life. With this considered, when it comes to making the move, it's your decision that matters.

It's your happiness that's at stake. It's your budget that's going to determine where you can go, and what you do. It's your dreams that are going to create a new, fulfilling vision for the life you want to live. It's your work that's going to fulfil your ambition and bring new opportunities and clients your way.

Just imagine if the perfect house came up in rural Scotland, and your best friend talked you out of moving. Two years later, her husband is relocated to South America, and you're left living in Birmingham. You don't air your concerns about her move, but you do have to watch her Facebook photos flag up adventures in the jungle and days spent by crystal-clear seas, while your dreams of living in rural Scotland remain exactly that, dreams.

I would encourage you to ask yourself what's the benefit of not relocating. What's the benefit of staying stuck where you are right now? What is the benefit of keeping your children in a school they don't like? What's the benefit of being close to family even if you hardly see them? What's the benefit of pleasing everybody else?

Not making this move might keep everyone else happy, but the next time you head to Zoopla and see the house of your dreams is under offer, I'm pretty sure your heart will sink, and you'll feel disappointed in yourself, and we don't want that.

When family and friends offer unwanted input, smile and thank them; trust your gut; and, regardless of what anyone else has to say, remember this is your life, not theirs.

Relocation exercise

Write down a firm statement about why you're moving and the reasons beyond this. Make it short and sweet, and memorise it. Then, if someone tries to talk you out of what you're doing, you will have your answer ready to deliver. Be strong, you can do this.

What Will You Miss?

While social media and mobile phones make keeping in touch easier than ever, there will be things you miss about where you are now, if you do decide to take the plunge and relocate, and this sets the doubts creeping into your mind at 4 a.m. when you're mulling it all over.

I'm not just talking about the people, although you could be moving to get away from relationships and friendships that are less than positive. As humans, we are formidable creatures of habit, and those little things in life that are so often taken for granted could be the little things that make your heart ache when you first set up somewhere new.

I know that while being in Devon has brought much joy to my life, there were small things that were part of my old life that made me feel a part of things, like a smile from the barista at my local Starbucks, and my coffee already steaming and waiting for me on the counter. When I rocked up in Exeter, no one had any idea who I was or that I always ask for a large skinny latte with two sweeteners – and that kind of stung. I didn't miss the people sitting in the coffee shop, I didn't miss the busy high street, or the drivers fighting for free parking spaces, but I did miss the familiarity of belonging. Today, I'm a regular in new places that gradually have become *my* places. And, yes, that latte is waiting for me, along with a cheery 'Good morning' and 'How are you?'. This took time to build and there is still a part of me that loves the anonymity the move gave us, but ask me to go back to the town I grew up in, and there is no chance I'd go back to that way of life.

This may seem like a simple question but making a list of what you would miss about the life you have now can be pretty telling, and could quell any doubts that are lingering.

Think about the people you'll miss, the sports or work team you're involved with, or the neighbours who are always there when you need them.

Write down the great things about where you live that you love, such as the shops; the beautiful Art Deco cinema where you can have dinner as you watch a classic movie; the bakery that sells the best cupcakes; or the coffee shop where they know what you like before you even order.

This simple chart doesn't look like much, but getting down on paper what you'll miss, what you won't, how you can deal with this situation and what this will free you up to do, can have a massive impact and leave room to successfully start over. You can also add this into your relocation journal and as you move through the process of starting over, it could well be these columns change and you start to see why putting the doubts in their place was a really good idea.

What Will I Miss?	What Won't I Miss?	How Can I Deal With This?	What Will This Make Space For?

What about Family?

Do you have close relationships that you'll miss if you move? What about the support you may provide to an elderly family member – is there someone who can step in and offer the help you have given for many years?

Then there is the support you might get from your family, such as childcare. This is something that can absolutely make you doubt what you're doing and put a shadow over making your next step the success you want it to be.

Joanna March says, 'The biggest thing I missed were friends and family.' This is a sentiment that Luisa Robertson echoes: 'I miss my friends and family most, [and] being able to ring someone for an impromptu coffee or playdate. I also miss having familiar comforts or places to go. Every day out is an adventure but there's something comforting about having favourite places to go. And the other big thing for me is missing being close to the sea – the nearest coast is about an hour from here.'

All these things matter, and your ties might make the doubt feel all the stronger, but it's up to you how much they should be counted as part of your decision to move.

Yes, you might miss people, but you can of course use social media to keep in touch. They can visit and you can visit them. While it might not be the same as living round the corner, it's really important to go back to the overarching reason why you're making this monumental decision, and check in with that every now and again.

Happy and Sad Leaving

Claire Lyons, a well-being expert, knows a lot about leaving and loss and says, 'When we move to a new place, whether our dream home by the sea or into a care home, we inevitably leave somewhere. Leaving "home" for many is a wonderful and exciting time. You may be leaving a place you have outgrown, or moving from a family home to your own place of independence; moving from being alone to being with others or vice versa. Whether you're happy or sad in general about the move, you do need to deal with the leaving and likely feelings of loss. If the move is not wanted, not positive or not to a place you feel good about for whatever reason, that feeling of loss will be even more acute.'

Happy leaving

If you're moving on from a place you've loved, there may be feelings of loss in emotional terms and powerful memories of important times. Think about ways to preserve some of those moments, perhaps by making a small video, taking photographs, or making a scrapbook full of memories.

If there are people from the area you would like to stay in touch with, remember to collect emails, phone numbers and other contact details before leaving, or set up an online group you can all access in some way.

Make a map of the area listing favourite places, people or buildings. This creates a fun way to return in the future and reminisce, or pass on to the next generation. You can mark changes each time you visit.

It may be possible to keep something physical from the space as a memento (please only do this with permission). Ideas could include a plant, piece of furniture, childhood lampshade, key, plaque with the name on, etc.

Sad leaving

If you've been forced to leave, or are doing so after a major life event, such as a divorce, bereavement or illness, and feel unhappy about it, it is even more important to work on coming to terms with the loss.

Think of your favourite element of the space and how you might capture the essence of that to reimagine in your new home.

Create a memory box: a space in which you can keep photographs or other tokens of your time in that home to reflect on later. This may be something others can help you with.

Try to allow yourself to view your new home as an opportunity. It's not the fault of the building that you're now there, and projecting that pain on to it will make living there even more uncomfortable. Allow yourself to be sad. It's a perfectly reasonable reaction to loss. Maybe keep a journal about your previous home, memories and stories.

Be clear about why you're going and when the doubts are shaking your belief, just go back to that idea and see if those worries are bigger than the life you're trying to create.

Chapter Twelve

Moving Without the Mayhem

I don't think there's ever been a moving day in the history of relocating that's been stress-free, but you can do your best to minimise the mayhem, so things go as smoothly as possible.

It's key to remember that, just as you might have a chain when it comes to your home, you're also dependent on other people doing their jobs, so your planning can go, well, to plan. This can be frustrating and stressful, but I'm afraid that there are some things that you simply can't press fast-forward on. If you try to do so, you could end up feeling overwhelmed and anxious, and no one wants that.

As a mortgage adviser, Phil Leivesley sees this a lot, and says, 'Don't stress about the time it takes to move. When you've found your new home, and your mortgage and plans are in place, try not to stress about how long it will take. Even if you're responding to queries from your solicitor in a timely and efficient manner, you have no control over the speed of the other side's solicitor and your vendor. So don't stress over what you can't control. It will usually take longer than you think so accept that and you'll alleviate some stress.'

I'm sure you have a timeline, perhaps a new job to start and those all-important school places to secure by September, but you having a meltdown won't do anything to make others go faster.

Make a List

I didn't want to write a book that was just about admin, paperwork and checklists, because I know that there is so much more than this when it comes to taking your life, family, possessions, hopes and dreams from one place to another – but an element of organisation is needed.

Even the most organised of us will drop at least one ball while planning a move and that's fine. Let's face it, packing up your life isn't a walk in the park, but a list – or rather many lists – will keep you on track and help you to successfully pack up and start over somewhere new.

Not only will your lists help you to keep calm, but being able to see, at a glance, what's been done and what is outstanding will stop you rerunning things in your mind when you wake up at 4 a.m. in a panic that you haven't redirected your post.

Debs Aspland, an organisation guru, says, 'Grab a new notebook or start a new folder on your phone's notes app and start a master to-do list. This is a place to jot down everything that springs to mind. You can move these notes into different lists as you progress but having one place where you can add notes without having to worry about categories or timelines is really helpful.'

Claire Lyons adds to this by saying, 'I had a list to fill in with everything I needed to know. I carried it in my bag and filled it in as I met people and found new things, like the doctor, dentist, pharmacy, bookshop, etc.'

Relocation exercise
Now is the time to take Debs' advice: start a master list and each time something new pops into your head, add it in!

Declutter Like a Diva
Whether you're going from studio flat to maisonette, boat to barn conversion, flat to farm, or from the family home you've loved since you had your children to a retirement home, you probably won't want to take everything with you, and you might not be able to take it all, either.

The school reports from when you were twelve, the teddy your first boyfriend won at the fair and those back issues of *Smash Hits* might hold a special place in your heart, but all of this stuff can add up. It can not only drag you down but also add to the cost of moving, and then sit in boxes under the stairs for months when you arrive at your final destination.

One thing that always catches me out are the greetings cards I've accumulated over the years, and I bet I am not the only one. While you might want to keep hold of every single birthday, Christmas, Mother's Day, anniversary, good luck, wedding and Valentine's card you've ever been sent, that soon mounts up into a lot of cards which are simply gathering dust and maybe keeping you stuck in the past. Sorting through these over a glass of wine, keeping the best ones, the most sentimental ones and those from people who are no longer here by putting them in a binder or scrapbook, not only saves space for things you really need, but can also be a great way to set your mind free from the past so it is ready for your next adventure.

A tip from Jo Henderson is, 'Be ruthless and only take what you really need! We took so much that the kids couldn't bear to be parted with and some boxes were never even opened!'

Olivia Heyworth, creative director and owner of property management company Heyworth Gordon, has some great advice when it comes to getting the clutter sorted and your move under way.

Declutter before a move

Moving an overstuffed junk drawer or closets full of stuff you didn't even know you owned doesn't make sense. If you move yourself, you'll have to pack and schlep all those extra things; and if you hire a removal company, you'll pay more to move junk you won't want in your new place.

Give yourself time

Don't wait until the day before the movers arrive to decide what to pack and what to get rid of. Instead, plan at least two weeks in advance. Mark out a few hours a day to tackle a different room or closet in your home. By working in smaller chunks, you won't be tempted to just throw it all in boxes and be done with it.

Use up extras

If you stockpile household goods and toiletries such as toilet paper or shampoo, start using up the excess now so you'll have less to bring with you. If you run out, buy a smaller size to get you through the move.

Start a necessities box

A necessities box includes everything you'll need the day you move in, such as a roll of toilet paper, a box cutter, a hammer and nails. Mark the box and keep it with you while you move so you can dive right in without digging through all your boxes looking for a necessity.

Use three boxes

For every room you tackle, bring three boxes: one for stuff you'll keep, one for stuff to throw away and one for stuff to donate or sell. As you go through closets and drawers, drop each item into one of the three boxes.

Employ the practicality test

If you're not sure you should keep or donate something, ask yourself – honestly! – if you'll use it. For example, set a time limit for clothes. If you haven't worn something in a year, you probably won't wear it again, so put it in the donation box. With sheets, towels or kitchen utensils, check for duplicates. While it might be nice to have three sets of sheets, one or two will do. The same goes for hand towels and spatulas.

Donate or sell

Once you've finished digging through every room in your home, either sell what you don't want or donate it to charity. You'll finally be rid of that clutter, and you'll make a little bit of cash (or a tax deduction) to help offset your moving costs.

Who's Going to Move You?

Some people pack up their lives themselves, others get professionals in to do the job; how you do it is up to you, but a little forward planning, cost analysis and foresight will help ensure your relocation goes as smoothly as possible. We know that it probably won't all be plain sailing, but there are things you can do to make it as pain-free as possible, and one of the main factors is to try not to take it all on yourself.

If it's just you who's moving, maybe you can do it yourself, but if you're a family of five going from London to Lincoln, or taking your brood from Bourne End to Boston, you might be best placed to bring in the professionals. From packing up your possessions to dealing with large American-style fridge-freezers (you won't get one of these on top of your Fiat 500), putting pianos on transit vans, and unloading in the rain at the other end, removal companies are more than worth the investment.

Ruth Walker has moved many times, and says, 'I moved once with five kids in tow, and a husband overseas working, and the movers left us at our new home with no beds built and all of the wardrobes in pieces – it was an absolute nightmare! Their excuse was that they'd never been asked to rebuild the furniture at the other end and had run out of time because they had another job to get to, so always be specific with the brief and get the essentials right to save time and tears.'

Asking around for recommendations is always a good idea. I'd say choosing a firm based where you live now is preferable to booking one based where you're going – but that's your call, and if your company is organising this for you, let them take over.

Once you're armed with recommendations and have checked out websites and reviews, get three quotes. You may want to have these with and without packing options – let's be honest, packing up a house takes a long time and it could be worth them doing it for you, especially if you're leaving work and tying up loose ends.

As well as looking at what possessions you've got to go with you, when companies visit they'll want to know about access to the property, your moving dates (which could change), and details for the new property such as narrow roads, steep driveways or slim staircases, and then they'll give you a price based on all of this.

Don't forget to have the quote in writing, ask for all terms and conditions, payment details, how many people will be there on the day, what time they will arrive, how many vehicles they will have, and check their insurance. Insurance doesn't just cover broken and lost items, but can help if there's a delay on the day and you can't get into the new property – this does happen.

Fiona Chow says, 'I was heavily pregnant and moving from Wandsworth to Hertfordshire. There was a police helicopter overhead as we were packing. I thought nothing of it until they sealed off the area, trapping our removal van at the storage facility up the road and me with half a flat full of furniture. [The house sale] completed at midday, but [there was] nowhere to put our stuff until about four in the afternoon.'

Helen Mary moved in the first week of the UK COVID lockdown in 2020, and says, 'It was a nightmare! Our funds didn't clear in time but fortunately our sellers allowed us in! We spent the whole day in the car with our daughters, nothing was open to use the loo or get food. According to my eldest, it was the worst day ever.'

When you're happy with your final choice, get them booked in and send them a brief. This might sound OTT, but it's fine to send them a briefing sheet listing fragile items and valuable objects, notes about large pieces of furniture that need taking apart and reassembling at the other end, whether the light fittings are staying, and what to do with white goods. It's worth writing rooms on each box because who wants to search 101 boxes at 11 p.m. in a new house, using a torch because the power has tripped? Not you.

How to Pack

Once you've sorted out the clutter, you can start to think about packing. Don't underestimate how long this takes, so getting ahead of the game is key to a stress-free relocation. It might feel that living in boxes weeks before you're going anywhere is premature, but having to pack the night before, running out of tape and smashing your favourite wine glass because you're tired won't help anyone.

Having packed more times than I care to remember, I know it can be a time-consuming, soul-destroying process, but a necessary one. Bearing that in mind, and the fact that you don't want to pile endless bags for life into the back of your car on moving day, I have some tried and tested tips to help make this job more manageable.

I wholeheartedly recommend that you clearly label all your boxes and bags so you can easily identify what needs to go where. If you're using professionals, they'll do this, but make sure you brief them so you're on the same page. You don't want to end up with all your kitchen goods downstairs, if you're moving to a townhouse with upside-down living.

Clothes
You don't need to take all your clothes out of the drawers; leave them in situ and secure them in place with wrapping, or be eco-savvy and use sheets or towels. Keep the clothes in your wardrobes on hangers, then put them in a wardrobe box, which will save you time, keep them crease-free, and you can use the makeshift wardrobes until the real ones go back up.

Breakables
A successful move isn't about smashed glasses, chipped mugs and broken perfume bottles that overpower your senses and ruin your handbag. Bubble wrap and packing paper have a place in the moving menu, but for a more accessible, sustainable option, wrap breakables in socks and use towels to pad out fragile, difficult-to-wrap items, like frames and vases. Wrapping knives and dangerous items in tea towels (double wrapped) could prevent an injury and a trip to A&E on moving day.

Prevent spillages
A successful start to a new life isn't unpacking to find your toiletries, make-up, cleaning products and detergent have exploded en route.

Make sure the caps are screwed on tightly, then put into bags (sandwich bags are ideal and can be reused once rinsed), and then put them into a sturdy box to be placed on the lorry – not under a heavy box of books or there will be tears before bedtime.

Ruth Walker adds her advice: 'Chances are you're going to have food left over, despite an endless mission to use everything in the freezer and ditch the out-of-date tin cans. Have a supply of insulated freezer bags (Lidl was a godsend when I moved) and make sure you or the removal men know where the food is when you get there – you don't want your Ben & Jerry's to be that last thing out of the removal van, and you certainly don't want to be hunting for the coffee!'

Wheel the heavy stuff
Wheelie suitcases are relocation lifesavers when it comes to packing heavy items like books, photo albums and heavy kitchen items – you can thank me later for that tip.

Take photos of your tech appliances
My husband and sons are tech-lovers, but even they take photos of appliances before they are unplugged to ensure they know where all the wires go when we touch down at our destination. From computers and fridges to TVs and the Sky box, you might think you know what goes where, but when you're tired, the kids need an Xbox fix and you want to post that first-night selfie, it's better to have a point of reference than a mutiny and meltdown.

If you're weeks away from going anywhere, or you have a very fragile chain, you might not want to pack everything, but having an idea of what's going where, and when, can help you to feel in control at times when you feel like you're surfing waves of uncertainty.

This can be even more helpful if you move countries and there will be a delay in seeing things. Debbie Favell says, 'It took three months for our things to get from Hertfordshire to the prairies of Canada, so we had to plan what we were going to need and what we could wait for. The bonus is that when it does arrive it can be a bit like

Christmas when you unwrap your belongings – you also question why you bothered to bring some things.'

You can take photos of the insides of boxes before you seal them up and you can number boxes and put rooms on them for the next place. This can help jog your memory when you can't remember where your hairdryer is, which box the kids' school shoes are in, or where your trainers are because you need to go out for a run and clear your head.

None of this is rocket science, but it's best to get things in place to ensure the move goes as smoothly as possible.

Animals and Moving

I've moved with pets many times and know this can be hard, for them and us. Travelling to Devon with a dog was easy, she had a lovely breakfast, a walk and a wee before we left and slept all the way. The cat, on the other hand, was a nightmare and thankfully our vet helped us with her.

Ellie Cavale from Vets on the Common in Clapham Old Town, has some great points so you can get your furry friends from A to Z.

Relocating with cats

In contrast to dogs, cats are more attached to their environment rather than their owners, i.e. it is more upsetting for a cat to lose its favourite spot by the feeding bowl than to lose its usual 'human butler'.

Relocating can create a lot of psychological upheaval for cats and indeed cause physical symptoms (e.g. stress-induced cystitis/urinary bladder inflammation). However, bear in mind that most cats have already relocated in early kittenhood, when they moved from the breeders to the new owners, so ultimately they learn to cope with a change of environment. There are several tricks to minimise stress.

Introduce any anticipated changes into the daily routine before the move. Ideally, indoor/outdoor cats will need to be kept indoors in the new location (ideally in one room for a couple of days). So it is a good idea to reintroduce a litter tray and confine the cat indoors a few days before the move.

On moving day cats must be kept in one quiet room away from all the upheaval. Then, when everything is packed away and delivered at the other end, cats can be moved into a quiet room in the new location, along with their favourite toys, blankets and feeding accessories.

There are several jokes about having to put a cat in a carrier for a reason. It's definitely easier said than done. From the cat's point of view, getting pushed into a small container is completely unfamiliar to them, or, worse, reminds them of trips to the vet. To avoid carrier stress, get the cat carrier ready. A routine of feeding or playing in the carrier, lined with a familiar blanket, is one of the best ways to integrate the transfer vehicle to the cat's life. For multi-cat households, cats rarely take comfort from each other when they are stressed – it's better to have one carrier for each cat.

It's very important to line the carrier with an absorbent layer (a puppy pad or lots of newspaper under the blanket) as a cat's bladder holds a large amount of urine, and stressed-induced urination or defecation is very common.

Once in the new location, confine cats in one room for a couple of days, then allow them to have the run of the house for two to three weeks (until they feel comfortable indoors). The length of adjustment is different for each cat – some feel at home after a couple of hours, some take a week to adjust; best to play it by ear. Once cats are happy in their new house indoors they can be allowed out.

Relocating with dogs

To begin with, consider your canine friend before you make the relocation decision. Is the new place suitable for dogs? Is there accessible outdoor space for them to carry on with the routine they are used to? Is there difficult access, such as steep stairs, that they may not be able to manage on a daily basis? Going from a house with a garden to a second-floor flat is not impossible for a dog, but it will take a lot more getting used to, and certainly you have to make sure that there are no physical restrictions that will make it difficult or painful for them, such as old-age arthritis.

In my experience, dogs are very much like toddlers, always looking to their human parents for reassurance and comfort. Better yet, during relocation, think of yourself as the travel agent organising a trip, or the cabin crew of a plane. A travel agent should be reassuring, but you would start to worry, rather than relax, if your travel agent kept calling you every two minutes to make sure you're fine. Likewise, in transit, you feel reassured when the cabin crew announce that there is mild turbulence and you should fasten your seatbelt, but, imagine the crew fretting, hovering over the seats, asking you how you feel and looking super worried about your welfare. You would start feeling stressed, right?

You would start thinking, *If the cabin crew are worried there must be something seriously wrong they are not telling me about.* Firstly, be reassuring but do not fret. Try to anticipate any alterations to the dog's routine before the move. You could try visiting the new location, or a similar one, like a hill or a beach, if this is what you anticipate will happen once you move. Try introducing in advance any new people or dogs that will be part of their new life. Taking their favourite bed, blanket and toys with you goes without saying.

On the day of the move dogs are better off away from the movers. Ideally, take a long walk with them while the household is being packed and unpacked (or have them go out with a familiar dog walker or friend).

Once you have arrived, try to be available for a couple of days to be with them to help them feel settled, but remember tip number one: do not fret! Be with them when they meet the neighbours or their new dog walker. Allow them time to sniff everything in their new vicinity, without rushing them to get from A to B. Think back to the slow, inquisitive walks you used to take with them when they were puppies. Unless, of course, your dog is

Mr or Mrs Congeniality and everywhere is home!

From a medical point of view, talk to your vet about the move, ask advice about any herbal or conventional medicines they recommend to help reduce stress during the move. Pets are more likely to go missing when in an unfamiliar environment so update their microchip details straight away (see your vet to implant a microchip if they do not already have one).

It is very important to find and register with your new vet in advance. Proximity and accessibility is the best criterion when choosing a vet, but, of course, read their reviews or ask pet owners in the new neighbourhood for recommendations. In an emergency, you need to know exactly where they are, their out-of-hours provision and they need to have your pet's records on file, especially if there are any ongoing medical conditions. Also, your new vet will advise you if there are any extra precautions you should be taking for local problems, such as tick protection where ticks are endemic, additional vaccinations where needed and so on.

Although it is normal for pets to be a bit under the weather in a stressful situation, seek medical advice if you see any unusual behaviour, e.g. frequent or lack of urination in cats or inappetence, diarrhoea or constipation, or excessive drinking in both cats and dogs. All these symptoms may be attributed to stress, but stress can also reveal pre-existing conditions that can deteriorate very quickly if left untreated. Cats are more likely to get into territorial fights in a new area; dogs are more likely to lose their recall and cross a busy road in an unfamiliar environment. In all the above situations, a trip to the new vets may be necessary, so ideally you should be familiar with their location (and driving route) well in advance.

Last, but not least, if the planned relocation is international, speak with your vet ahead of time, at least two to three months beforehand, to find out all the legal requirements. Depending on the country of origin and destination there are several procedures (vaccinations, parasite treatments and blood tests) that need to take place well in advance so that you have all the necessary documents on the day.

Boom! It's Time to Go

With the goodbye party a slightly fuzzy memory, your last lunch has been eaten, tears have fallen, and the removal lorry is ready to go, things will feel real. Your final day could be fraught if you're waiting for solicitors to do their work and for your chain to complete, but once you have the green light, it's going to be all systems go.

We all like to think that moving day will go smoothly, but the reality is that there can be solicitor delays, broken-down removal lorries and lost keys, so it's best to be prepared.

Jo Laybourn knows only too well about this, and says, 'Having paid for a removal firm to pack all my stuff and drive it to the new house, when we got there, my solicitor told me the move could not happen that day due to monies further down the chain. I agreed that the people moving into my old place could stay there as they had a small baby and nowhere to live that night! I had to stay the night with my parents, who luckily lived near the new house. To help with my move, my stuff was driven back to the removal firm depot in Kent from Surrey, then returned the next day, when I got the keys! The extra storage costs (£600) were covered by the people in the chain who delayed the process!!'

Lynsey Sizer adds, 'We moved twenty-four hours before the twins were born. As we arrived with the key, they were still moving out. The weather was boiling, and I was struggling. They then told us the mice problem they were supposed to sort hadn't been sorted. Also they hadn't emptied the garage, or the ponds, as agreed. I could go on, but it was quite a day.'

You might not want to be as unlucky as Natalie Komis: 'I've fallen down and up stairs three times whilst moving, resulting in hospital visits on moving day and badly sprained ankles or damaged ligaments. Once I broke both elbows in a cycling accident the day after moving. All my stuff was still in boxes, and I'd just moved in with new housemates who had to help me go to the toilet; we became good friends after that.'

To ensure things go your way, on the day you need to be prepared, and to start working earlier than the night before you move.

Before you leave, I'd suggest you do the following:

- Turn off the appliances that are staying at the property and take final meter readings (and snaps). I know I've mentioned this already, but if the next family is arriving the same day, you don't want them showering or cooking dinner on your bill!
- Make sure children, teenagers, elderly family members and pets are safe and accounted for – yes, really! You don't want to get halfway round the M25 only to realise Nibbles is still in her carry case in the utility room.
- Double check all cupboards. Only when I wrote this book did I remember the time one of the members of Little Mix came to look at my house. In a bid to have it looking perfect, I went into tidying overdrive and at the last minute I stuffed a pair of kids' shoes in an unused cupboard; only now do I realise I didn't ever take them out. Thinking about this, it might be a wise idea to keep cupboard doors open once you've emptied them so you can see what has been packed. If this isn't practical (small fingers, cats going to sleep, toes being stubbed and OCD tendencies), putting a Post-it on doors that are done could work. This can be the same for bathroom cabinets, kitchen drawers and storage boxes, and can offer peace of mind, but I'm sure you will check everything again. Twice.
- Passports, tickets and money aren't just for holidays, they're vital to a house move, so check, check and check again that you have these, as well as all important documents and keys.
- It's a really good idea to pack an overnight bag just in case things don't go to plan and you can't get into the carefully packed necessities box marked 'First Night'. Keep it with you in your car. Emmie Lou adds to this, saying, 'Pack a suitcase for each person who is moving, especially if you're going to be working once you've moved. Take a bowl with you, for water for your dog while you're on the road.'
- Do a double-check of the house, garden and garage, or be out of pocket like Jen Melor who told me, 'I left all my Christmas

stuff in a loft of one house and only realised the following Christmas when it was too late – LOL.'
- Flush all toilets before you close the door for the last time. Need I say anything more?

I don't know how far you're moving, but on your journey be sure to take plenty of breaks, use a satnav so you know you're on track, keep your cool and remember why you're doing this if things don't go to plan.

Good luck and see you on the other side!

Relocation Tip

Make sure those last bits – aka your necessities box – are taken from the kitchen and packed with you for the journey and your first few hours somewhere new. That's the kettle, tea and coffee, sugar, milk, mugs, as well as toilet and kitchen roll, dusters, cleaning products and snacks – snacks are VERY important. Pamela Spence comments, 'It is not unusual to find that your energy dips for a while after you've gone through all the excitement of the move. This is just your body recovering from all the excess stress hormones. Try, if you can, to take time out each day to rest; make sure your diary isn't too full; and that you're eating regularly and well. At this time, it can be helpful to take adaptogenic herbs like Ashwagandha (particularly if you have disturbed sleep and any anxiety) or Rhodiola (particularly if you need stamina). These herbs are becoming more common over-the-counter products as herbal companies learn about their effectiveness in helping recover from stress. If you're buying pre-made remedies, make sure you buy from a well-known brand, so you know exactly what you're getting.'

Chapter Thirteen

It's a New Dawn, It's a New Day

There's something exhilarating and liberating about the moment you close your new front door, take off your shoes, and breathe in deeply as you realise YOU DID IT!

I feel like I should be calling round with a bottle of fizz and a moving card, but if I was to do that for you, I'd have to do it for every reader, and I could get kind of busy!

What I can say is, 'Congratulations!'

You relocated somewhere new, and I've got utmost respect for you. I hope you can see just what you've done and how much you've achieved.

I know that for some of you, this moment will feel amazing. For others, it will be a mix of sadness and relief. It could mark the end of a marriage you didn't want to leave, or the start of a relationship that you feel is for keeps.

Maybe you've got a new job that you start tomorrow and are super excited, or the school gates are beckoning your little ones and you're feeling apprehensive about them making new friends.

It could be that you're reading this in the home office you hadn't envisaged working from, but your partner needed to relocate for their job, meaning you're finally free to follow your dreams, too.

Whatever the reason, and wherever you are right now, well done. I'm so proud of you and excited for what's next on your adventure.

Take a Breather

Stepping into my halls of residence in Leeds, arriving at my house in Tokyo, unpacking my clothes at my first London flat and crash-landing at our seaside home in Devon are special memories for me because they signified I'd made my relocation dreams come true.

These moments need to be savoured and treasured, so can I suggest you put the kettle on, make a brew, get the biscuits out and just take a few minutes to observe what you have done?

Years, months, weeks, days and hours of blood, sweat, tears, anxiety, worry, concern and deliberation will lift from your shoulders as you sit down (on the floor if you can't get to the sofa) and look at what you've achieved since first picking up this book.

Yes, there are still boxes to unpack, toothbrushes to find and people to meet, but for now, just be with your new space and breathe in the sweetness of relocation success.

Celebrate Your Success

I really do ask you to celebrate your relocation. It's a big deal and a major life change that needs to be marked accordingly, so don't let it pass by as if it's nothing. It's massive.

After waving off the removal company when we got to Devon, we had crab sandwiches and champagne at our local pub on the beach, and while it was drizzly (remember, lots of rain) and the ice machine was out of order, it was one of the best, most poignant, emotionally fuelled lunches I've ever had.

Knowing we'd defied the odds and left the doubters to doubt, we celebrated our new life by the sea. It was an utterly liberating moment and I'm sure that if I could bottle that feeling, I'd be a very rich woman.

The question is: what are you going to do to mark this monumental moment?

It could be a party if you've moved closer to family and friends, a swim in the lake at the end of your road, a cup of tea in the garden you've dreamt of for years, or a long hard cry to let out all those feelings that have kept you small and stuck for so very long, before a glass of fizz to seal the deal.

Anica Rosenberg told me, 'I stared at the stars in a clear sky, it was so unlike Camden. I remember the Big Dipper being the first constellation I pointed out to my son – bare feet on the grass, clear sky, and the cool fresh air of the night. An unforgettable evening, and we've never looked back.'

Heidi Scrimgeour told me, 'My son was three at the time of our relocation and had never seen the new house. We moved from North London to the northernmost tip of Northern Ireland, via six months at the in-laws' in Scotland, but when we finally pulled up outside after an epic journey sailing over the Irish Sea, he ran straight up the path and shouted, "We're home!"'

Nicola Buckley moved to Cornwall, and says, 'I walked on the beach and my family came over for prosecco on my new balcony as we watched the sun set.'

You don't have to be totally unpacked to celebrate your move, and Georgina Walker, who has moved many times with her military husband says, 'We usually celebrate with a bottle of fizz, sitting on the floor, waiting for our furniture to arrive ...'

Not all celebrations are popping corks, and Asher Benjamin adds, 'I bought myself a painting when I found out I got the job that brought me here, which fits the bill as a celebration, and I've made a point of putting it up on the wall as soon as I can in each of the many houses I've lived in since arriving in Portugal.'

Lauren Malone, adds, 'In March 2019 we moved. I was eight weeks' pregnant and had just quit my job and officially started my business. The first night in our new home felt like a new chapter had really begun. We sat in the garden and listened to the silence and quietly celebrated everything that had got us to that point (even the burglary that spurred our move) and everything that was to come.'

Leah Eser gives further insight into seeing just what she achieved, and says, 'When I arrived, I had a big cry and a "What have I done!" moment, but I picked myself up, went to explore and marvelled at the fact I'd got on a plane and moved to Asia.'

What you do to celebrate your move doesn't really matter; it's simply noting that you did it that's so powerful!

Relocation exercise

In your relocation journal, write down how you will celebrate your relocation when you arrive. You don't need to tell anyone else, but I'm pretty sure that when you sip that G&T overlooking the sunset you've wanted all your life, you'll look back and think, *Wow, I did it.*

Cheers!

Getting Used to Your New Home

Home is a feeling, not a place; isn't that so very true?

The success of your relocation isn't going to be based on how big your house is or how swanky the local shops are, but on the way you feel about being there. You've done a lot of the hard work and now it's time to decompress, unpack and prepare for a fabulous new chapter in your life.

Go for a Deep Clean

Really deep cleaning a new home is great not only for hygiene reasons, but also for your mindset. One house we moved to was filthy, and in the three years we were there, I never got that original musty tang out of my head, even though my fingers were raw from all the bleach I used to clean it.

Living in dirt isn't great, and when it's someone else's filth it can gross you out, so a deep clean inside and out could help you feel fresh and bright. Whether you do this or you pay a cleaning company to do it for you is up to you, but clean inside the cupboards; check out the state of any remaining appliances, especially the fridge and oven; dust away the cobwebs; scrub the bathrooms; clean the windows, inside and out; throw away or wash curtains or blinds that were left; and even check the state of the garage and shed.

This might sound a bit much, but a clean start is a successful start, so get out the cleaning materials you so carefully packed, put on your favourite music and clean your new home so it feels like yours.

Unpack at Leisure, not Pace

If you're anything like me, the moment you step inside your new home you'll want to unpack *everything*, while also stripping the gold wallpaper in the hallway and cooking a banquet to ward off moving-day hunger pangs. From experience, cut hands and a terrible post-move hangover when dinner turned into a fizzy affair isn't the happiest, most productive way to start a new life.

I know you might think there's an urgency to get things set up the way you want them, but giving yourself permission to let go, and allowing those around you – be they partners, children, elderly relatives or the cat – to do the same, is a sensible, kinder way to go.

Getting IG-filtered photos of a perfectly unpacked pad might be driving you to do more, but you don't need to do EVERYTHING on day one. Seriously, you do not! Yes, the neighbours might come round to say hello and bring goodies, but they won't judge you on the number of packing boxes you still have in the kitchen, and if they do, well ...

Yes, make it feel like home, but that doesn't mean unpacking every box, wheelie suitcase and portable wardrobe that's calling your name to be emptied and put away. Take your time, get a feel for your new space, explore the rooms and work out what will look right, where.

Putting pictures on the walls (check your contract if you're renting), putting throws and cushions on your sofas, getting photos out and using the same diffusers and cleaning products you had at your old home can help bring a sense of normality to somewhere new, and calm any post-move chaos.

Joanna March says, 'One tip I picked up was to have a colour wall that follows you – paint a wall in that colour as soon as you can and once your comfy chair, sofa, cushions, throws, pictures and photographs are placed in front of it, then you can replicate home wherever you go.'

Kathrine McAleese adds, 'Getting family photos up and my favourite blankets out starts the process of settling into a new home. Once I have the kitchen set up, with a decent shop done, I can relax.'

The kids having their toys around them will be comforting,

putting the dog's bed in the kitchen will make it feel familiar to them and you, and lighting your favourite candles will bring an instant feeling of being home.

Make your beds, put up curtains and blinds to keep the light out at night, and try to keep to the same sleep routine as before the move. Pamela Spence suggests, 'If sleeping in your new home is taking a while to settle, try to surround yourself with familiar things in your new bedroom. This is a common issue but one that should pass relatively quickly as you get used to your new surroundings. Lavender oil is very helpful here – a couple of drops on your pillow can help you nod off much more easily. Don't overdo it, though; too much lavender can be a bit stimulating, so don't be tempted to spray it everywhere! Avoiding caffeine after lunchtime will be helpful too, and adding in a sleepy-blend herbal tea just as you're getting ready for bed will help set you up for the night. A traditional hot, milky drink can be really useful here too – if you don't do dairy then use oat milk instead. Both contain a chemical called tryptophan that can help improve sleep. Adding sweet spices like cardamom, cinnamon and even turmeric makes a delicious bedtime treat.'

After moving into your dream home, a sense of newness can last for months – especially if you were in your last place for a long time. This is a marathon, not a sprint, and trying to do it all at once could lead to tempers being lost and tears being shed, meaning you may not start your new life on the high you had expected.

Unpacking your boxes doesn't mean you'll automatically feel settled, especially if your busy routine means you haven't been able to spend time connecting with the space around you, but it's not unusual to feel this way, and it won't last for ever! I'm sure that in no time at all cups will be left on the table, dirty clothes will fall on the bathroom floor, and shoes will be scattered by the front door, making it feel just like a home from home.

Olivia Heyworth has some great tips on getting to grips with somewhere new.

Simplify your new space

After a few months in your home, if there's anything you haven't put to use, be honest and ask yourself if you really need it. Having unused furniture or unpacked boxes lurking in the spare room can be a constant reminder of the upheaval you've faced, or make it feel like you're getting ready to move again. Give those things away, recycle them, or put them in long-term storage. As a bonus, there will be more room for the stuff you love!

Grow things

It's amazing what the addition of a few plants can do, both in the garden and inside the home. Planting and looking after a few living things, whether they're exotic flowers (for the more green-fingered) or cacti and succulents (for the occasional waterer), can both make your space cosier and give you a sense of control and responsibility over your environment.

Give your walls some TLC

It's surprisingly easy to put off decorating for a while, then not get around to it at all. Take a deep breath and put a day aside to get it all done. You'll find that hanging your favourite photographs and paintings, or even things like cleverly displayed ticket stubs and dried flowers (anything with personal memories attached), instantly injects personality and reminds you that this home is your own.

Reassess your property

Once you've been in your new home for a while, be honest – is there anything that doesn't work for you? If you keep walking into the sofa, shift the furniture around. If there's not enough space for chopping vegetables in the kitchen, think about getting a kitchen island. Anything that might make your space more liveable is a bonus, and now you know the property better, you're in a great position to make it work for you.

Remember, nobody's home is perfect from the moment they pick up the keys, and it can take a while for anybody to settle in. It will happen in its own time, probably without you even noticing.

Making the Kids Feel at Home

If you're moving with children, get them to unpack their toys. You could make their beds and unpack their clothes, as this means they can start to claim their space and feel more settled. You might not want My Little Ponies all over the place as the removal men try to unload, or books and games on every surface, but the kids will be experiencing a range of emotions (and raging hormones in some cases), so having a secure base and the familiarity of 'home' will be key to them feeling settled.

Let them Facetime old friends and grandparents from the word go, make sure you take time out of doing jobs to go exploring the new neighbourhood, and when wobbles happen give them reassurance, answer their questions and remember, no one is too old for a hug from Mum and a big bowl of ice cream.

Do Your Admin

I've mentioned this, I know, but make sure your paperwork and admin are up to date. This will not only ensure your affairs are in order, but it'll give you the headspace to focus on the fun things. From changing the address on your driving licence and updating your bank accounts, to ordering new bins and sorting the council tax, it all needs to be done, so set aside an afternoon and cross each task off your list.

Register with a GP

This is important, and we didn't do it, so when my son ran into a marble table on week two of our seaside relocation, it wasn't good. You might think you won't need a doctor, but you never know, so don't let this fall to the bottom of the list. Instead, register as soon as you can, and add members of your family too. It's not a bad idea to check out where the surgery is, along with A&E, so if you fall off a ladder as you're fixing the gutters, you know where to go. Oh, and do the same with a dentist!

Cover the Basics

Having a 'go to' hairdresser, gym, bakery, butcher, florist and pharmacy somewhere new really helps you to feel like you're at home. They sound like small things, but being able to have my nails done, go to a coffee shop on the beach where they started to know my face, and even finding the cinema helped us tick that 'we are home' box.

Have Fun Exploring

Just as you need to get your home to feel right, this is the time to check out the lie of local land, and that can be so much fun. Yes, you will have boxes to unpack, and a massive pile of ironing to do before work starts, but make sure you get out and about as this will remind you why you moved, something you can lose sight of if you stay within the confines of your four walls all day.

Remember when we talked about visiting and using that time to check out the good and the bad? Well, now is the time to go out and explore everything else. From the local boutiques and bars to museums and galleries, beaches, bike tracks and swimming pools – go for it. You moved for a better life and new experiences, so make sure you take advantage of all of those things, and so much more.

Olivia Heyworth agrees with this sentiment and adds, 'Enjoy a stay-cation. If you're out and about all the time, put time aside for a holiday at home. Plan some activities in your local area, enjoy a few lazy mornings, and cook (or order) your favourite food. If reading on the sofa is your thing, do it – or if you're more interested in watching a box-set marathon, go for that instead. Consciously spending time at home, rather than using it as a place to hang your hat, is the easiest way to feel more at ease in your new place.'

Relocation exercise

Using your relocation journal, write a list of the things you want to do in your new area, where you want to go and what you have found that you love. Put it on your fridge door to remind you why you're here and how it feels to explore places that in the past were just ideas in your journal. When you go to those places, why not take a photo, collect a shell, keep a ticket and use this to make a memory picture you can frame and place in your new home?

Don't Get Stuck in a Rut on Day One

On day one you might find a great Chinese takeaway because it's on your road and you were too tired to cook, but this likely won't be the only place to get food from, so check out all that's on offer around you. It could be that six months in, with a heck of a lot of pizza, pasta and sushi eaten, the Lucky Star sweet and sour chicken is still the best of the bunch, but at least give other things a go.

After five years in Devon, we still try to do something new once a week. A swim in a lake on Dartmoor, ice cream on Blackpool Sands, or swimming at the uni pool in Exeter are all on the list, and with so much still to explore, we'll never get bored. However, we could get lazy if we didn't stretch our sights further than a five-mile radius. Plan ahead, get things in the diary, and I love posting photos on Facebook not only to share our adventures, but it means each year there's a handy reminder of all we've done, how much we've achieved, and how successfully we started over. Go on, I dare you.

Map It Out

Navigating somewhere unfamiliar, whether it's big or small, is tricky at first, and it can take trial and error to work out one-way systems, find shortcuts and get to grips with slow tractors or fast trains. Yes, you can use your satnav, but driving around, taking buses, as well as walking the streets helps you get to grips with your new location. Take your time, study maps, and if you get lost, who cares? You might end up somewhere even better than you had planned.

Expats in Touch

I was an expat in Tokyo, and it was tough, but knowing I had a tight-knit expat community to turn to, thanks to connections from family and friends, was really helpful, especially as I was twenty-two and far from worldly wise. I'm sure you'll want to find your own way in Seattle, San Francisco or Sydney, and make local friends, but established expats will welcome you in, share hints and tips, and be a part of your journey. From finding supermarkets that sell Heinz Baked Beans, to advice on what the best painkillers are and how to fill in your taxes, getting help from those people who have been there and done it could save you time, blushes and gain you a new bestie.

Leah Eser says, 'I'll caution you that expat life is not as glamorous as one might think. There's a lot to deal with: leaving your home, family and friends, and culture shock to name a few. I would say it's key to do your research. Search for Facebook groups – 'Two Fat Expats' and 'Grumpy Expat' are full of people who live all over the world. Someone is bound to have experience of where you're moving to, so you can ask for top tips or advice ahead of the move. If you need to find accommodation before you leave, these are good places to get recommendations for any realtors or estate agents that are trustworthy. Googling blind can be a little risky.'

Social media groups are a good place to start, and you can look at those before you even step on the plane, as well as apps like ExpatBuddy. Before you go, do a call-out to your network – you never know who might have a mate in Madrid, a friend in Philadelphia, or a cousin in Cancun.

Start a Tradition

Every Christmas Day since we arrived in Devon, we've gone to the beach before tucking in to turkey and roast potatoes. Rain or shine. Wind or hail. We pop to our favourite coffee shop for a cuppa and mince pies, and watch people in the sea, horses on the sand. One year Santa rowed right past us in a little red boat. For as long as we live here, it's something we'll do, and I hope one day we'll do it with our grandchildren bashing buckets and spades, high on the excitement of seeing Santa by the sea.

I'd invite you to create a new tradition of your own, be that running around Central Park on Sunday morning, having champagne at The Ivy on your birthday, or sitting by the lake near your home to mark each year you've been there. Find something that resonates with you, and I hope that ritual will create a foundation for your successful new start.

Give Yourself Time

After relocating, you'll adjust at your own speed, so please give yourself the time, space and compassion to get used to being somewhere new. Finding a coffee shop that makes the best flat white, making a friend at work, knowing the kids are happy at school, and having a wicked pizza delivered on Friday night are all things that will help you feel at home, but these take time to find, so enjoy the ride.

Glennon Doyle is famous for penning the term 'We can do hard things', and if we give ourselves time, and credit for our strength, this is so true when it comes to relocating and successfully starting over.

Leah Eser is testament to this. She says, 'I settled much quicker than I thought I would. I spent three months before my move to Singapore dreaming up the worst-case scenarios and worrying about leaving my home and family. Leaving my mum at the airport was hands down the hardest thing I've ever done. I remember getting through security and just bawling my eyes out in Heathrow, wanting to turn around. But I got on the plane, and, honestly, I've been stronger ever since.'

There are no deadlines for fitting in, no magic number of weeks before you won't wake up and wonder where you are, and no one is watching from the sidelines to see if you've made friends, got a promotion, or are having second thoughts about moving, no one. You're here to successfully start over, so take the pressure off and enjoy the ride.

Four Seasons in One Day

You can think about settling somewhere new as a year-long process. It doesn't matter which month you move in, but from day one, look at how the seasons change in front of you as a way of truly experiencing somewhere new.

I talked this over with a friend recently and she said, 'I used to lust after my neighbour's gorgeous cottage garden because it was beautiful and full of colour. When a new couple moved in during the winter, they immediately cleared out all the plants which, in that season, weren't looking very exciting. By spring they had completely replanted the garden, which must have cost a fortune. Although it looked lovely by the summer, I felt sad for them that they never knew how wonderful it could've been if they'd just waited.'

Watching the summer sun set over the horizon, the leaves changing from green to golden red in the autumn, feeling the crunch of frost under your wellies in the winter, and seeing spring bring fresh life into your garden can be pretty magical. It can put you in touch with somewhere new in a totally different way.

Maybe it's going to take the changing of the seasons for a full year to help you to settle – just a thought.

Chapter Fourteen

When the Honeymoon Period Is Over

I'm writing this book as we hit our five-year anniversary in Devon and, I'll be honest, I still feel like we're on holiday most of the time. With that said, the initial feeling of euphoria will start to die down as you adapt to your new life. As you drag the bins down a slippery drive on a cold February morning, you might wonder what you've done. But don't worry, that's natural and just another part of this process.

When we moved here, not for one moment did I think we'd made a mistake, but when, eight years earlier, we moved from London to the Home Counties, the experience was very different. In a matter of months, I'd gone from having a fabulous career to being a mum to a baby with a milk intolerance, in a new town where I hardly knew anyone, and when I saw photos of my London friends having riotous fun in Soho, I felt sad and lost. However, as I found my parenting groove, my son moved on to solids and my partying pals sobered up, it didn't feel so raw. But if I I'm honest, it was only as we drove down the M5 to 'south-west freedom' in 2016, that I felt like me again.

Whether you're going to university, relocating to further your career or are on a family adventure, you might feel less than excited once the initial high dissipates, but that doesn't mean you've made a mistake. Yes, some people will have got it wrong, but in most situations, it's simply a time of transition. Things will settle, you'll start to feel at home, find friends, and if it does get hard, remember your reason for going in the first place.

Expecting to feel at home in a matter of days isn't realistic. Enjoy the ride, be true to your feelings and go at your own pace.

Dealing with Homesickness

If you're reading this with a gin and tonic in your hand and tears streaming down your face because your husband is still at work, you don't know a soul where you are, but your old pals are out partying, please know this is 100 per cent normal. Homesickness for where you were can rear its pesky head for quite a while.

Getting out of the house, visiting those places on your wish list, walking around your new neighbourhood, saying hello to people you pass on the street (this is so easy if you have a dog to walk), and having coffee in a local café are all ways to forget about what was, and live for the moment, even for a little while.

Keeping in touch with those you left behind will help you keep positive on the days when you're wondering what you've done, but at the same time, don't get so trapped in the past that you can't let the future in. This is the time to look forward to the new, so embrace where you have gone and see the good in your life right now.

Resentment about Moving

When your relocation was driven by someone else, be that your boss, partner, children or parents, you may be angry, sad and downright mad about finding yourself in a situation, and location, you didn't want to be in. Moving might not have been on your agenda, but bottling this up won't be good for you. Sitting on misery and resentment could impact all elements of your life and relationships, which isn't going to help make this a success, even if you don't want it to be a success right now.

Don't be ashamed or afraid to feel your feelings and talk them over with someone you trust; by doing this you'll hopefully be able to accept where you are now and not hate everything about it. If you don't talk it over, it's inevitable that there will be snappy moments with those you love and live with, which could escalate into an argument where things you don't really mean are said, but can't be taken back. Relocating might not have been what you wanted, or maybe resentment is being thrown back at you for instigating change, but as time goes by, friendships are made, your house becomes a home and you find things you enjoy, and could come to like. For now, sit with those feelings, give it time and be kind to yourself and those around you.

If you're really struggling with the changes, maybe you need to talk things over with a professional, so do some research. Remember, there are many online options out there today, but please don't do this alone, as it could lead to anxiety and depression.

If you can, try to think about any positives this opportunity brings you, and look at the new life you can create if you're open to change and adventure. If that means you get a part-time job to meet people, join a running club to get those feel-good endorphins pumping around your body, or take a yoga class at the village hall, go do it and have some fun!

Time is a healer, and it will get easier.

Grief and Relocating

Just as there is grief when you lose someone you love, the same feelings can bubble up when you relocate, making settling in really hard. When I left London, I grieved for my career and carefree life for a long time, but this made me feel selfish because I was newly married, had a beautiful baby and a gorgeous home. It doesn't matter who you are and what you have, grief can hit you like a ton of bricks when you relocate, and that's okay, but, what's not okay is to push this aside and smile like everything is postcard perfect. If I'd talked about my feelings when I felt this way, maybe I wouldn't have been so unhappy about a move that was meant to be so full of hope and joy, but, instead, baby blues were kicking the buggy wheels as I tried to walk my way out of grief.

Laura Toop is a grief and loss specialist, and has some great tips that could help you if you're at a loss for what to do when you aren't as happy as you thought you were going to be somewhere new.

Let go of 'perfect'

It does not exist; it never did and never will. You cannot control or predict every eventuality which may play out, it is not humanly possible.

Pace yourself

Everything does not have to happen on day one, nor will it, so be realistic with your expectations of what is feasible in a day. Remember, perfect doesn't exist! As humans, we are woefully inept at short-range planning, so focus on only one big task in any one day, or three smaller ones, and you will better manage the curveballs that can and do arise.

Focus on what matters most

What is most important now? Act on that, and only that. Yesterday is gone, and tomorrow may not happen, so it's only now that matters.

Have a 'support strategy'

Identify the things that might stop you from achieving what you want to happen. What support can you request or put in place to ensure it does not stop you in your tracks?

Remember there is always, always a way forward

Take a pause, step away from the situation; there will always, always be a way forward. Focus on visualising what it is you want, not the how, because a new how will present itself.

Visits from Family and Friends

For some people, seeing loved ones from their previous area is a comfort; for others, it could make them miss them even more and leave them feeling worse. Geography and costs will play a role in how often you see those you left behind, but that's the whole point: you didn't leave them behind. You just started over, and you now have an entirely new chapter to share with them.

As well as catching up on the phone, using Facetime and Zoom means you can actually see people in real life (well, as close as it gets), so if you've always had a family roast on a Sunday, or a catch-up after the school run on a Wednesday with a friend, do it virtually and keep the connections strong. I mean, you can't pass the gravy through an iPad screen, but you can share stories from your week, laugh at Dad's terrible jokes and admire your bestie's new trainers. See, it's really not that bad.

If your parents used to look after the children in the holidays, maybe they can stay with them for a week or two instead, and no one says you can't jump on a train in Bristol on Friday night and be with your London mates for last orders and a kebab.

The more you can see this as the next step in your life, not a horrific loss, the easier it will be. When you embrace the new, the more fun you will have with those you miss when you do see them, and it's really amazing to be able to show your family and friends around your new neighbourhood, waving at the neighbours as you walk by. That's actually a really lovely feeling and is great confirmation that you did the right things, and are successfully slotting in somewhere new.

Bear in mind people will be missing you too, but they'll want you to put your roots down and make friends, so don't put this new life on hold and jeopardise its success by living in the past.

Relocation exercise

If you're missing loved ones, start planning visits back to see them, or meeting up halfway for dinner, as well as organising Christmas and birthdays so you have dates in the diary and things to look forward to. But I warn you, as you settle somewhere new and time goes by, this might become a bind and your diary will get full of fun stuff with new people. Just give it time.

Navigating Culture Shock

Far from being nonsense, culture shock can be a very real experience and dismissing it can be damaging.

Starting over anywhere new takes time, but when the weather, language, food, dress codes, social roles, values, customs and even basic communication methods (I covered my mouth when I laughed for about six months when I came back from Tokyo) are added into the mix, it can take even longer to adjust.

Culture shock might not kick in on day one, but as the subtle nuances of daily life – everything from attitudes towards women to differences at work – are uncovered, a feeling of unknowing and not believing you belong can come along and knock you sideways. This often happens in a new country, but it can also occur when making a regional move – I remember feeling the north-south divide when I went to uni, and that was just a 200-mile drive in the UK.

If culture shock is impacting how successfully you're settling in, these ideas could help ease the pain and get you back on track.

Be open-minded

Being open-minded and trying new things in an unfamiliar environment is important, even if it feels wrong and goes against your values. For example, as a woman you may have to cover up when you go outside. You're somewhere new, so get the most out of the experience, rather than judging it; find out more and make an informed choice. I felt slightly out of place in rural Japan, but people were interested to know about me and about English culture (they often asked me if I knew the Queen), and while being stared at freaked me out, I gradually got used to it and saw they just wanted to know more.

Interact with the local culture and people

It might feel hard to get to know local people, especially if there's a language barrier, but the more you do that, the easier your transition will be. Making friends with locals, going to restaurants and bars, as well as learning the language are all key to integration. You may well be surprised at how much people want to welcome you in. There might be rules and regulations, depending on where you move to, so be aware of these, but getting involved is going to help you feel less alone and isolated.

Ask questions

If you don't ask, you don't get, so if something is confusing you, ask someone about it. This could be face to face, in a local shop, at the library or on an online forum. If you're afraid of standing out in a different culture, this won't change if you keep yourself to yourself, so embrace the new and get to know what's going on around you. Most people will want to help, and asking for that can be a game changer. If you're too shy to ask, read about it first, educate yourself, and then take the plunge.

Try new things

If wearing a kimono, eating with chopsticks, not drinking alcohol, giving your neighbour a high-five or bowing when you meet someone new is what happens where you've moved, give it a go. You might feel awkward and out of place to start with, but if you want to start over successfully, getting to grips with the culture is key and will serve you well.

This will take time, so don't give up at the first hurdle, and when you do get it right make a note of it so you can see that you can do this!

Be Aware of Depression Setting In

For some, feelings of anxiety and depression can be very real when moving somewhere new, so look out for this in yourself, as well as with family members and partners. Being separated from family and friends, having a lot of admin and jobs to do, settling the kids into school and starting a new job, or not having one to keep you busy, can really impact your mental health.

Debbie Favell says, 'When we got to Canada, my sons settled brilliantly and so fast. They took everything in their stride and made new friends immediately. I, however, found the lack of friends very hard and lonely. Just being with a toddler all day was tough, and I felt that I lost my identity somewhat. It was hard learning the ropes of a new country, not knowing what things were called or where to get things. Six months into the move I experienced depression and it was a combination of feeling lonely, grief, loss, guilt and losing my identity. Since moving to Ontario I have made a really close friend, like I finally found my person.'

If you feel like you're becoming trapped in a cycle of doubt and unhappiness, at a time when you were expecting to be elated, just stop and look at what's going on. Be mindful of your feelings and remember that bad days happen even in Hawaii, so don't be hard on yourself. Having a new routine in place, getting out of the house, taking exercise and eating healthy meals can all help you to keep on track.

With all of this said, let's not diminish the reality and severity of mental health issues. If your mood doesn't lift, and you've spoken to someone you trust about it and you still don't feel better, check in with a professional and see if they can help you. This won't be for ever, but while you aren't feeling great, get the support you need, and you'll be glad you did.

Social Media and Mates Back Home

Anyone who knows me knows I love social media. Had Facebook been around in 1995 when I was in Tokyo, things would have been easier. A shared phone in my apartment and a fax machine at work, along with letters, were my main points of contact with the outside world. Had I been able to send WhatsApp messages and set up Zoom calls with family and friends, I have a sneaky feeling I might have stayed out there for longer, and that Christmas Day spent teaching Japanese students how to order a burger and fries might not have felt quite so lonely. Today it is easier than ever to be closer and more emotionally connected, however far away you might be physically.

If you're really missing your mum and dad, speak on Skype once a week, and I'm sure the kids will love sharing stories of their new school and the fabulous friends they've made. Even if you're in California and your sister is in Cardiff, I'm pretty certain you'll know what she had for breakfast and what colour her new trainers are, thanks to her Instagram feed and Snapchats early in the morning, or late at night as you grapple with the time zones.

Perhaps your former colleagues are on a work night out and you still feel like the odd one out at your new office, but, hey, you can see the photos and hear about the mishaps, all while not having to endure the hangover the next morning or the red face when you see your boss in the staff kitchen.

I know it's not the same as having that person there with you in real life; you knew at the start of this process there would be sacrifices. However, a lot of great things could come your way. When homesickness and loneliness kick in, go back to the vision board you created, remember the soul-searching you did before you signed on the dotted line, and look at the new friendships and memories you're creating.

Focus on the Positive

Getting lost on the way to school, your post not being redirected to the right address or your new tenants defaulting on the rent might make things feel hard, but focusing on what's going well will help you settle faster. Joining the gym, being invited to your neighbours for a BBQ or watching a stunning sunset are all signs that you're in the right place and you're starting to make this home. No one said this was going to be easy, and there is no fairy godmother who can click her sparkly heels and make everything okay, but give it time, and the magic will happen.

Plan Treats

You're somewhere new, so make sure you're going out, exploring and finding the people and places that could help you settle. Trips to the cinema, shopping at the farmers' market, going out to buy some new rugs for your home, visiting a different pool or getting out into nature will all help you to feel like you're at home, so make a list, put things in the diary and stick to them.

Relocation exercise

Every day, make sure you write down three good things that have come your way and put the pieces of paper in a jar in your kitchen. This could be finding a pair of slippers you thought you'd lost during your move, making a friend or spotting a robin in your garden. Big, small or hardly there at all, these bite-sized wins (including getting to grips with the culture shock mentioned earlier in this chapter) will keep you on track. If you're having an off day, pick a few from the jar to remind yourself of just what has gone well.

Chapter Fifteen

Building a New Network

Whether you're moving from a large city to a small town, or from a village to a sprawling metropolis, feeling like you're part of a community takes time and effort. While it won't happen overnight, it will happen eventually.

Each time I've moved, I've left a circle of friends and had to start again. This is something I was happy to do, and it means I have connections around the world that I cherish, but some are no longer on the radar, and that's something I have had to make peace with.

Try not to be hurt or surprised if some friendships start to fizzle out, and don't always think that you have done something wrong or upset the other person. Just as your life changes in your new location, so does theirs, and if you aren't bumping into each other at the school gates or the water cooler together, you may well grow apart.

Social media makes keeping in touch with those people already in your life easier than ever, but if you put in the time and energy, and have faith you can do it, you'll make new connections and friendships will flourish.

It is important not to think about making new friendships as starting over from scratch, but instead see it as an extra layer in your existing friendship and support network. This is about where you are right now and the people, groups and clubs that come into your life will further enhance the connections you already have.

Naomi Breese McKiernan further comments on this by saying, 'Making friends is so much easier if you have kids or dogs. But you have to approach a new relocation with the attitude that you're prepared to work at it. That can be uncomfortable and unrewarding, especially when people already have their friends and don't recognise how hard it can be to move and find new friends. It requires a really open perspective, you have to be open to all sorts of options and be willing to invite and ask people to join you, which is sometimes difficult.'

Jo Henderson concurs with this, saying, 'You have to change your mindset and become a "joiner-iner"! We made friends through the school during our second relocation to America, and the first time we were out there, we made friends through work. In both cases we had to be more involved than we would have been at home.'

There is no doubt that making new friends takes effort and time. It can take you way out of your comfort zone, but the effort is worth it when you get a hug at the school gates from a new friend, an invite to a party or a birthday present dropped at your front door.

I know that this will be a breeze for some people reading this, and that is great, but if the idea of being vulnerable and opening yourself up for potential rejection fills you with fear, I have some ideas that might help.

Be Choosy

Some people will tell you to say yes to every invitation that comes your way, but on reflection I'm not sure that is the best tactic. You know yourself best, and if you're going to thrive in your new location, you need to do what feels right for you.

I'm a self-confessed introvert, so for me to accept every invite for coffee, drinks at the pub, walks on the beach, networking or school PTA meetings, my anxiety would go into overdrive and rather than making solid connections, I'd talk way too much and absolutely overshare. Yes, I will go to events, but not one every day, and I know that a drinks party in Exeter with other business owners would energise me on the night, but the next day I'd plan to be in my office, writing and drinking coffee, on my own.

It's nice to be asked to go to things when you arrive somewhere new, but don't feel bad about saying no. There will often be more invites to come.

Go to the events and invitations that appeal the most to you, see what works and what doesn't, what the people are like and if it's worth investing your time going again.

Say Hello to Your Neighbours

You might still feel raw after leaving Sarah and Andrew next door, Kirsty and her cute puppy over the road, and you really miss Harry and Clive's fabulous Friday cocktails, but you'll have new neighbours – even if your nearest ones are a mile away in the Outer Hebrides! – and there are friendships and connections to be made.

When I work with coaching clients, we often talk about tackling the easiest options first when it comes to starting something new. Given that, in most cases, your neighbours (aka potential new friends) are on your doorstep, why not suss them out first and see if there is a fit? Even if this is out of your comfort zone and you don't want them in your house every day, Ramsey Street-style, it can be helpful to know your neighbours on some level.

Eve Menezes Cunningham found this when she moved to Ireland, and says, 'I landed in heaven when I moved here, and even before I moved in, I was so lucky with the neighbours. The first popped by to introduce herself when I was painting before I moved in. She came with homemade jam and bread for me. Some have become good friends and I value and appreciate all of them. [They are] so kind and welcoming.'

Sally Todd agrees with the local camaraderie, adding, 'It sounds a bit stalker-like, but when I saw neighbours out chatting I'd pop down to empty the bins, say hello and then we got chatting. One particular friend lives alone and so I offered to help when she needed DIY things as we had ladders to reach the high ceilings. We are now great friends and meet up for coffee and lunch, and chat by text. I also joined our residents' association in order to get to know more people where we live.'

For Debbie Favell, it was her accent in a new country that broke the ice: 'When we moved into our house (that we bought having never actually set foot in it) our neighbour on one side was a ninety-something-year-old lady originally from England, who came round and introduced herself. I think she had heard our accents, and she knocked on the door the evening we were unpacking with a tray of freshly made doughnuts and a welcome-to-the-neighbourhood note. We now exchange Christmas gifts and have each other's telephone numbers.'

Whether you need to borrow a cup of sugar, have someone keep an eye on the house when you go back to see family friends, or need to know where A&E is when your child has a fall (that might have been me), getting to know the people who are close by can be a positive step towards not only making new friends but settling into a new area and feeling connected and part of the community.

Kathrine McAleese makes a great point when she says, 'Try to find the local post office, corner shop and pub, as they likely have noticeboards with news about local events. When I go in I always get chatting to people because establishing those loose social connections really helps.'

Sharon Thompson adds to this sentiment, saying, 'Going out of your way to shop locally and making conversation whilst you do is a great way to get to know people, and if you have children, local mum-and-baby groups are a good place to start making friends.'

Join a Club or Group

Being a part of something bigger than you can be a great way to establish yourself, find a new friendship group and gain a sense of belonging.

If you're reading this book and are starting university, being able to join a club or group is part of Freshers' Week and something you'll automatically get to do, but if you're a little older, you'll have to do the groundwork for yourself.

Social media helps you to see what's out there, with many

groups and clubs having their own Facebook pages and groups, so do some research and see what the options are. If you've moved to the sea, how about finding a swimming club or paddleboarding group? For golf fans, the local club is a great starting point, and joining a gym can be a brilliant way to find people with similar interests and likes.

Helen Bawden found her place in the community through the choir, saying, 'For me it was finding a group where I knew I'd then find people with the same main interest as me. I found a local chorus choir. That first evening, as I sat listening to them, I finally felt that I had found home. I went on not only to sing and do concerts and singing competitions with them – winning a bronze medal in Ireland – but I became their Deputy Director. As I say, the first night I visited them I finally knew I was home.'

Francesca, who moved to Andorra, also joined a choir to make friends and adds, 'Make contact with as many relevant groups as you can to find your people. I assumed I would meet people via my son's school, but my closest friends here I've met in different places. I quickly engaged with an expat group and found some good friends through that, which helped a lot.'

Jo March says, 'For settling in after an international move I found using the local Google search engine helped get better results for local blogs, community pages and groups. I finally breathed out when I went to my first group lunch – I felt like hiding, but a kind woman shepherded me in and sat me with another newcomer. We then spent a few weeks meeting up and exploring the city together as our partners worked.'

Religion can also play a part in making friends, and this was the case for Kathrine McAleese, who comments, 'Lots of active churches also have house groups or community groups you can join to get to know a few more people. That also then means you have people you see about the town to say hello to. Now you're not an outsider or stranger, now you have at least a handful of people who know your name, who you can say hello to, who'll ask about your family and how you're settling in. Even for simple things like knowing good local tradespeople to bring in, it's been crucial for me, not just for my faith, but for quickly settling into a new environment, whether that's a new city or a new country.'

If you have children under the age of four who are not yet at school, you might want to go to as many library story times, toddler groups and forest school sessions as you can, both for friendships and your sanity.

Working for yourself when you move means you'll need to build your business as well as your friendship circle, so going to coffee mornings and cocktail parties could boost your visibility and, in turn, your workload.

The key is to try things out, get a feel for the people, see if you fit in. If it feels like a good fit, go a few times; if it's terrible, then don't go back. Generally, there's no way that after one Zumba session you'll leave with a whole bunch of besties, but give it time, show up week after week, break the ice and, after a while, you'll have the friends you deserve.

Volunteer

Volunteering can be a fantastic way to get more involved in your local community. As well feeling good about giving something back, you might make lifelong friends, and, who knows, even get a job. Whether you make tea after church on a Sunday, read stories at your children's school or spend an afternoon as a guide at the local museum, this can give you purpose as well as the chance to socialise and settle in.

If you moved as part of your retirement or are newly single, volunteering is a brilliant way to build your confidence and find people you really connect with both when you're on duty and when you're off. You will be part of something bigger than your family unit, you might get some much needed company if you moved on your own, and it could even spark romance. Many local Facebook groups, websites and even the library will have opportunities, so give it a go; you never know, an hour here and there could lead to a lifetime of love and happiness.

Kids and Friends

Just as you, the adults in this relocation equation, need to settle into your new home and work out the lie of the land in the neighbourhood you now find yourself in, your children are going to be exactly the same. It may take them time to adjust to the changes, and perhaps even forgive you for making them move.

Depending on their ages, where you moved to, and under what circumstances, the situation will be different, but I promise that you can do this.

For children and teenagers, settling into a new home and a new area, even a new country, can be a tough adjustment to make. Saying goodbye to old friends may well have been difficult, but the excitement of moving can sometimes reduce the initial anxiety they might feel.

When we came to Devon, we didn't know a soul. Because we moved here at the start of the summer holidays, we had six weeks to find our feet, work things out and get a feeling for life by the sea.

Siân Smith talks about this and says, 'Parents should make sure that they acknowledge the emotional difficulty of relocating their children and moving them away from close friends and social groups. Therefore, establishing networks and routines for actively staying in touch with close friends is fundamentally important. Even if that means that their child simply joins weekly Zoom dance classes and virtual, social meet-ups, or schedules phone contact at certain routine times each week, it is important that they actively encourage it. This will emotionally support their child and keep them feeling safe and secure, and ensures that at least 10 per cent of a child's comfort zone is being maintained, supporting them through the tough transition process.'

There are ways that you can help make this an easier transition, and Simon Lockyer, Headmaster at Royal Hospital School, comments: 'Preparation is key. Encouraging your child to get involved with the school selection process and going to the open days will all help them be in a good frame of mind about their new school from the beginning. Your child will feel well prepared in advance of them starting and this all helps to ease any anxieties. Look for schools that provide a welcome pack and go through it with your son or daughter to help manage their expectations and get any questions or worries answered before starting the new school.

'Talk to your child's tutor or house staff about any issues, challenges and personality traits in advance of them starting so that they know how to best support your child. And soon after you've made the move, revisit those conversations for their opinions on how your child is settling in. It's also important to choose a school with excellent pastoral care and mental health support so that it is available should problems arise. You can support your child in settling in and establishing friendships by organising playdates to reinforce new relationships. Also, encourage your son or daughter to try lots of new co-curricular activities which will boost their confidence and enjoyment within the school.'

Debbie Favell has four sons, and some sound advice: 'We had concerns about how the boys would adapt and fit into schools here in Canada, but ultimately they had no problem at all. The other kids liked them because they had "cool" accents (and royal names) and were from somewhere else. They slotted into the new routine perfectly. The parental aspect was difficult, learning how the education system works (it is different from province to province); some provinces have catchment areas, others don't, so that changes how you find a school. We found differences in the way classes are taught compared to the UK and we worried to begin with if they were at the right level. They made friends on the first day and soon felt like they were part of the furniture! Basically, we had to have faith in the process, and with regular checks with the kids and their teachers everyone was happy that they were exactly where they needed to be.'

Jo Henderson and her family had a similar experience with a move to California: 'I spent far too long worrying about whether my kids would be okay at their new school in the US, and then would they be okay once they were back in their new schools in the UK. They adapted brilliantly. Having said that, they are both quite clever and also are self-starters.'

There are a multitude of activities, clubs and sports you can get involved in, but that is going to be down to you and your children, and what feels right for them. I remember we would sign up for everything at school in the first year, only to find out the muddy way that a cycling race around the school campus in November probably wasn't the best way to make a first impression, but everyone was kind and cheered my nine-year-old son on to the very last tricky pedal.'

Don't Rush In

Remember when you started school and knew no one? How about those early days at college when you hid under a floppy fringe and tried to stay on the periphery? Maybe it felt tough in your new job when you would go into the kitchen and everyone else was chatting? Relocating is very similar, and in many cases you won't know anyone, but if you can see this as an exciting new chapter and a chance to choose your friends and be surrounded by people you like, who support you and inspire you, it can be a wonderful project rather than a terrifying experience you're subjecting yourself to.

When we first got to Devon we rented a house with lots of space, a hot tub in the garden and the most magnificent view, but it was set in a row of four houses on their own, between one town and another. Before long I felt it would be nice to be part of a community. I wasn't talking about the goldfish bowl of where we had previously lived; I was missing the chance to say hello to people as they walked past the drive or build a relationship with them in the local shop. Now that we are in the heart of a village we have that. Some of this comes down to planning your move; some of it is also reflected in renting before buying. I'm glad we didn't purchase that particular house as it simply wasn't in the right location, but I do still hanker for the view of the sea from the bedrooms.

I would say that walking is one of the best ways to get to know a new area and to get a feeling for the people you're now living in close proximity to and the community you feel you're going to be a part of.

Please remember that many people start over and have to make new friends, so take it day by day and know that the right friends will find you eventually. Oh, and once you're settled in, when someone new moves into the area, why not see if you can extend the kindness you received as a newbie?

It Only Takes One

Where you used to live you may have been super popular, on every email list, in all the WhatsApp groups and part of the social scene, but remember that was then, this is now, and all you need is *one* person to help you start feeling like you belong.

It could be someone in the library, a girl at work or mums at football practice who make you feel that connection. When we follow our instincts it often leads us to a happy place, and nurturing a potential bestie could be a wise investment of your time. Being brave enough to message them about having a coffee, sending a friend request on social media or simply waving and smiling when you see them at the school gates could be enough to find a friend for life.

It's worth noting that when you make new friends, they're likely to have a network of local friends who, over time, they may introduce you to, and, before you know it, those social butterfly wings will be used once again and you'll have found your place.

As Jo Henderson said so well, 'become a 'joiner-iner'. However hard and scary it might feel as an outsider, it could be your best move and lead to close friendships, great memories and a successful relocation.

Give things time, don't expect too much of yourself – or others – straight away and I am confident the right friends will come your way at the right time.

Relocation exercise

Start a new address book when you arrive at your relocation destination. I don't mean buy it on day one while your home is covered in packing boxes, but as you get to know the local shops, pick up a book and add details over the coming months and years. Yes, you can use your phone, but this simple task can give you a real feeling of connection, and you can obviously add people from the past as well.

Chapter Sixteen

When It Doesn't Go to Plan

Just because you set out with a spring in your step, a bikini in your bag and a belief that your relocation is going to work, there's no guarantee this will be the case, and there's no shame in admitting things haven't gone to plan. It's no mean feat to uproot your life, career and family and start somewhere new, and there's always the risk that it won't work out.

That's just life sometimes. But please don't feel that it's all been for nothing; you've given it a go and that takes courage, so well done.

I knew, in my heart, that leaving London as newlyweds was a mistake because I simply wasn't ready, and looking back I wish we'd stayed in Chiswick. However, hindsight is twenty-twenty – maybe today I'd be sitting on the board of directors of a PR agency had I not left London, not writing this book in a beachside café.

Lowri Dorrington says, 'We moved to the Bahamas in August and knew by Christmas it was only going to be a temporary move. We'd said two years but ended up coming home after one.'

Sarah Reis had a roundabout relocation which illustrates that U-turns happen. She says, 'We moved from London to Devon to follow our dream of running a country pub. The first six months were bumpy, and we worried we'd made a big mistake. We gave up the pub, moved to the coast, and have never looked back. We love our new life by the sea, our work–life balance has totally changed, we swapped our party shoes for hiking boots, are healthier, happier and have made some lasting friendships.'

Debbie Favell adds, 'Relocating certainly isn't for everyone and it doesn't have to be for ever. We set ourselves review points where we would discuss how we felt, whether things were working for us and, if not, what our options might be.'

Michael Padraig Acton talked to me about how to deal with post-moving regret. He says, 'This is a time to be reasonable with yourself, which is a very difficult thing for humans to do. When we've done something and we have regrets, it could be that we're not seeing where we were before through a clear lens; we may be wearing slightly rose-coloured glasses. For example, you may miss the home and the garden and your neighbours, but if you really think about it, was it as perfect as you're recalling? Were there issues you're not also remembering, and could it be that you're just not quite settled in your new place yet? So really pull it apart a bit, pull back the layers of the onion. Be honest with yourself. Look at why you moved and where you are right now and what can you do with that? What can you make beneficial and to your advantage? And what is it that you're really missing about the past and can you replicate that where you are right now?'

The Reason Things Don't Go to Plan

If you're reading this and know you don't want to be where you are, fear not; you aren't alone and there are things you can do.

My move to Tokyo was temporary, but just ten months in I'd had enough and went home. Maybe I could've stuck it out for longer, got a promotion, dated my Aussie flatmate and travelled more, but my heart just wasn't in the Land of the Rising Sun, so I had a rethink, took my cash out of the bank and never regretted doing so.

Missing people

Family dynamics and relationships can be complex, but for some people, being away from their nearest and dearest, even if they're now living in paradise, can be too much. Even in this fast-paced digital age, being physically close to those we love is more important than wall-to-wall sunshine, better than incredible working conditions, and beats being on a spin bike next to David Beckham in LA (well, actually, I'm not sure about that one).

If you're missing your mum and dad, grandchildren, best friend or neighbours, and loneliness is setting in, maybe it's time to have a rethink. There are no prizes for being miserable, and eating humble pie can be worth it if it means your happiness and mojo come back.

The wrong school

It seems like a lifetime ago now, but as my elder son was about to start Reception we made the classic new-parent decision to move house to get into a school. Yes, it ticked all the boxes when it came to Ofsted reports, SATS, and the 11-plus pass rates, but when it came to being part of a community, I'd never felt so out of place. We lasted a year and the day we left I felt relieved, if not a little foolish, but the longer we stayed the more I felt like an outsider and the more my son was misunderstood. I didn't want to admit defeat, but there are only so many times you can be judged and your child can be bullied, so my advice is not to leave it as long as I did, as it still makes me feel sick almost a decade later.

Cecile Blaireau comments on what to do when a school transition isn't smooth: 'Don't despair or feel guilty. Each child reacts differently, and it does not mean you're a bad parent. Keep being supportive and try to get involved as much as possible with your kids. Ask them questions about school. It will give you a good idea of their feelings. And communicate with the school, the teachers. The more you're a team with them, the more successful the change will be. Don't hesitate to ask for tips, advice or any help from the teachers. They are experienced and always happy to help. If anything, you will make their job easier by being a helpful parent. Hear their feedback even if it is not always easy to hear. And see how you can support them and your kids' learning.'

Siân Smith says, 'As a parent, your children not settling after a relocation could be your worst nightmare. However, there could be several reasons, and the difficulty is that children and young people can be notoriously difficult at opening up. They may not always know all the precise reasons why they are struggling to transition well. They may feel guilty for feeling less than perfect, especially when they know that their parents have undergone such a difficult and extensive move, and don't want to be responsible for putting additional pressure and worry on their parents. Alternatively, they may feel that they are "odd" or "problematic" for not fitting in. One way to investigate any potential problems is to contact the tutor, head of year or head of house at school to try and establish a virtual picture of the child's day-to-day interactions, and academic experiences in the classroom.'

This isn't the end of the world. While you may feel guilty about the changes you inflicted on your kids, they don't have to stay where they don't fit in; it just means you need to reassess.

When love turns to heartache

The heady highs of falling in love can lead people to make drastic changes to their lives, such as moving to be closer to a partner. The trouble is, if things don't work and you're left with heartbreak, debts, disappointment and loneliness, you may wish you'd stayed where you were. It might be that you gave up your home to move in with a partner, and when things go sour, you're effectively left homeless. Yes, this is sad, but you didn't have a crystal ball to see the future, and you thought you were making a long-term change for true love.

Use this time to work out where your next home will be. While you'll need to heal emotionally, think about what you learnt through the experience and the ways you can deal with things differently in the future.

When the finances don't add up

Moving is expensive, so when it doesn't work out and you end up in debt and struggling, it can really hurt on many levels. This is why it's important to do your planning and sums at the start of your relocation, and to not take on more than you can manage. Maybe you bought a project house that has cost way more than expected? Or Brexit played havoc with exchange rates and you're out of pocket in Poland. Or the school that seemed so nurturing had a bullying problem and now independent school fees are adding to your already slim savings.

All of these scenarios can spiral, and you can lose control of your personal finance, leading you to regret your relocation.

Moving to the wrong house

Yes, another classic mistake, and one I made. While a three-storey townhouse with a double garage, four bedrooms and en-suite bathrooms seems like a good idea in newly married bliss, with a baby, buggy and endless stairs, it wasn't right! We live and learn, but there can be regrets when you have bought a new house. If it doesn't feel right, it could scupper your health, happiness and peace of mind, leaving you hankering for your home.

Phil Leivesley says, 'It's worth considering whether you have a back-up plan if you relocate, and it doesn't work out. You might even consider renting out your current property for six months while renting a place in your new area, so that you can make sure it's right for you before committing in the long term. Renting is a good way to test the water. I also suggest you know what your long-term plan is where your mortgage is concerned. When do you plan to pay it off? Will you sell up and downsize? Or will you want to stay where you are? Try to plan for the future to alleviate any worry. A good broker can advise you.'

Don't Feel Bad

The common theme for all of this is that it is better to have at least tried, to have lived a different life in a new place and to see if it was what you wanted, than to keep wishing you had been brave enough to give it a go and never gone for it at all.

There is no need to feel bad or ashamed when a relocation goes wrong, but it is my duty as the author of this book to let you know that sometimes this does happen and there is a way out. Staying stuck when you know you aren't happy can be harmful.

Jo Henderson has a pretty philosophical way of looking at this kind of situation. She told me, 'Everyone who takes the leap and relocates but then returns home will always have their heart in two places. Now that we are back in the UK, we always say that we left half our hearts in California. It is a wonderful experience, but it expands your horizons to such an extent that you're always aware, at some level, of what is out there and what your other life – if you had made different decisions – might have been. On down days, I wonder if it was the right decision to have gone, as I am now always left wondering if we should have stayed in California. These are usually cold, wet, wintry days. If we hadn't gone, we wouldn't know what we are missing!'

Food for thought.

Just because your relocation looked perfect on paper, it doesn't mean the reality is the same. The worst thing you can do is deal with this on your own, or sweep your feelings under the carpet because things won't miraculously get better; they'll get worse. Call someone – whether it's your partner, flatmate, boss, or your mum back in Colchester – speak up, and, as they say, a problem shared is a problem halved.

If you really don't want to stay where you are, look at what's gone wrong, what you could do to find where will be right and get a plan together. Maybe even go back to the start of this book with a fresh pair of eyes and a belief that it will, one day, work out the way you want it to.

As Farah Radford rightly points out, 'Get out while you can. Otherwise you'll lose yourself in the process of having that "ideal life" that everyone thinks you should have and be so thankful for.'

No one is going to judge you if you decide that this hasn't been for you, so please don't judge yourself and stay somewhere that doesn't make you happy for the sake of saving face, because that could break you and be anything other than successful.

Chapter Seventeen

The Relocation Toolbox

I've covered a huge amount in this book, and while you may have bookmarked key pages, added notes and made lists, this one-stop relocation resource toolkit is intended to be a handy reference point for packing up and successfully starting over.

Books

Whether you go for a paperback, e-reader or absorb words by listening to them, not only will books (like this one) help you move, but they can also be a source of inspiration when it comes to decorating, organising your clothes, keeping calm, finding a new job or navigating networking somewhere new. Here are some titles that I've found useful:

- *The Complete Gardener* by Monty Don
- *Design the Home You Love* by Emily Motayed and Lee Mayer
- *The Little Book of Hygge* by Meik Wiking
- *Networking a Successful Small Business* by Joanne Dewberry
- *The Squiggly Career* by Helen Tupper and Sarah Ellis
- *The Life-changing Magic of Tidying* by Marie Kondo
- *365 Ways to Feel Better* by Eve Menezes Cunningham
- *Think Big* by Dr Grace Lordan
- *Untamed* by Glennon Doyle
- *Wherever You Go, There You Are* by Jon Kabat-Zinn

There are some great books that I've found for children that might help make your move easier to explain and make fun:

- *The Little Book of Friendship* by Laurie Friedman
- *Molly Moving* by Shirley Hughes (my favourite moving book ever)

- *Moving House* by Annie Civardi
- *Topsy and Tim Move House* by Jean and Gareth Adamson (my second favourite moving book)
- *My New Home* by Marta Altés (a cute book about moving house and making new friends)

If you're moving with older kids and teenagers, these books could come in handy. Leave them in their rooms and see if they show an interest, but don't force it if they are still coming round to the changes they might not want to make:

- *Being Miss Nobody* by Tasmin Winter
- *Go Big: The Secondary School Survival Guide* by Matthew Burton
- *New Kid* by Jerry Craft
- *Yesss!: The SUMO Secrets to Being a Positive, Confident Teenager* by Paul McGee
- *You Are a Champion* by Marcus Rashford
- *You Are Awesome* by Matthew Syed

Broadband

You never really know how fast and reliable the broadband is until you get somewhere, but a good place to start is the Broadband Speed Check (www.broadbandspeedchecker.co.uk). Make sure you ask your estate agent, as well as the owners of the place you're going to be renting or buying from, to get the real low-down.

Business Help

If you're going into business for yourself, or growing a side hustle when you relocate, these sites may help you get things off the ground:

- Enterprise Nation for hints and tips, www.enterprisenation.com

- Eventbrite for events, great for networking, www.eventbrite.co.uk
- LinkedIn is the place for business networking, www.linkedin.com
- Startups has a huge wealth of information about setting up a small business, https://startups.co.uk
- Talented Ladies Club has loads of information for female business owners want to make their ideas grow, www.talentedladiesclub.com

Candles and Diffusers

You'll probably have your go-to faves, but a sure way to make somewhere new feel like home is to fill it with love and great scents. This can also help deal with old odours that are lingering!

- Neals Yard, www.nealsyardremedies.com
- Neom Organics, www.neomorganics.com
- Space NK, www.spacenk.com
- The White Company, thewhitecompany.com

Careers Advice and Job Searching

Finding a new job isn't always plain sailing, but it can be fun and exciting, and these resources could be a good place to start your search:

- Guardian Jobs, https://jobs.theguardian.com/careers/
- Indeed, ukindeed.com
- National Careers Service, https://nationalcareers.service.gov.uk
- Reed, https://www.reed.co.uk/career-advice/

Crime Rates

I've mentioned crime and safety as something to check out *before* you move, and www.ukcrimestats.com is a great place to start, as well as local newspapers and their websites, social media sites and even the police department for the area you're interested in.

Education and Schools

If you want the lowdown on schools, www.goodschoolsguide.co.uk is an online information resource and a great place to start.

You can read Ofsted reports at www.reports.ofsted.gov.uk, but nothing compares to going to visit yourself.

If you have younger children and need day-care, both https://www.daynurseries.co.uk and https://www.childcare.co.uk are worth a look.

Zoopla has www.locrating.com for real-time school information that's pretty handy.

Gardens and Green Spaces

Whether it's a window box in Walthamstow, a pond in Peterborough or a vineyard in Versailles, outside spaces can be key to successfully starting over, so I've got some delights to tempt you.

Border in a Box is a brilliant independent business who send out ready-made garden border design kits that take less than a day to complete but will help set up your new home, www.borderinabox.com.

Homes and Furniture

There are so many options when it comes to making a house a home, below are some of my favourites:

- The Dulux Visualiser app allows you to test different colours to your heart's desire so decide before you paint! Find details at https://www.dulux.co.uk/en/articles/dulux-visualizer-app

- Habitat is an oldie but a goodie, and has some great pieces that add light and life to your home, www.habitat.co.uk
- The Hambridge Artist has a collection of seriously cool art that will give an edge to even the sparsest of spaces, www.thehambridgeartist.co.uk
- Freecycle is for you if you want to do your bit for the environment – give and take www.freecycle.org
- IKEA – www.ikea.com – need I say more? Same goes for John Lewis, www.johnlewis.com
- Oliver Bonas is brilliant for something a bit quirky that will make you smile on the days you're feeling less than chipper, wwww.oliverbonas.com
- Photo Measures is the perfect app to use to take photos and write dimensions on them, so you can plan where everything goes before you arrive. It could mean you lose bulky furniture before you even leave and that could lighten the load and ease costs.
- If you need some help with organisation, The Association of Professional Declutterers and Organisers are worth checking, www.apdo.co.uk.

Journals, Planners and Stationery

I won't even admit how much stationery I own and the number of journals you'll find in my office, but it's safe to say there's a lot. As I have mentioned keeping a relocation journal in this book, I've made some suggestions of where you can get some of the best ones.

- I love Clever Fox planners for work and they could help with your move as well as keeping all the plates spinning, cleverfoxplanner.com
- Dailygreatness sell outstanding journals, so check them out, dailygreatness.co.uk
- CGD are a funky London brand that have some fab journals and planners to keep you ahead of yourself, worth a look,

www.cgdlondon.com
- Going for classics, it's got to be a Moleskine journal and notebook, www.moleskine.com
- Paperchase are great for all things paper, www.paperchase.com
- For a little class, Papier has got you covered, www.papier.com
- Flying Tiger is a great shop for journals as well as a whole load of cool house stuff so totally worth checking out in person or online, www.flyingtiger.com
- *Happy Confident Me* is a gratitude journal for kids and could help with happiness, positive thinking and resilience when moving and is by Annabel Rosenhead and Nadim Saad

Magazines

Whether you pick them up at the local shops, flick through them at the library when you sign up, or drool over them online, magazines are fantastic relocation resources for ideas and inspiration. The great thing about paper copies is that you can use them for scrapbooks and vision boards, and I've listed some of the ones that I hope might have you reaching for the scissors and glue.

- *25 Beautiful Homes*
- *Amateur Gardening*
- *BBC Gardeners' World*
- *Country Homes & Interior*
- *Country Living*
- *Elle Decor*
- *Good Homes*
- *Homes & Gardens*
- *Home & Style*
- *Homebuilding & Renovating*
- *House & Garden*
- *Good Housekeeping*
- *Livingetc*

- *Red*
- *Style at Home*
- *Women & Home*
- *The World of Interiors*

Official Property Details

If you're checking out the lie of the land as well as rules and regulations, these are some of the top resources that might come in very helpful:

- For all things environmental, go to the Environment Agency, www.gov.uk/government/organisations/environment-agency
- Another government site in the UK is HM Land Registry, www.landregistry.data.gov.uk
- The Guild of Property Professionals is a great source of information and is the national network of independent estate agents. Details can be seen at www.guildproperty.co.uk. They also have online mortgage and stamp duty calculators as well as an online valuation option so you can see what your property is worth
- There's also the National Association of Estate Agents (NAEA) which keeps the industry working as it should and comes with a ton of help, www.propertymark.co.uk
- Many people look at properties that have the potential to be converted. If that's you, you'll need to check out not only the place you're hoping to buy, but also the local planning department. This isn't always an easy process; watch out for listed buildings and tree preservation orders, and be prepared to fork out cash and keep plenty of time for this. You can start looking at https://www.gov.uk/browse/housing-local-services/planning-permission and take it from there, but don't skip this bit or you might really come to regret it
- A decent surveyor is a must when you're buying and selling a property, so make sure they are part of the Royal Institution of Chartered Surveyors (RICS). Check out www.rics.org for

more details and if you need a local RICS surveyor, pop your location into https://www.localbuildingsurveyor.co.uk

- Some people aren't fans of mortgage calculators – remember, they are only as good as the information you give them – but if you want to get some starting figures, www.moneysupermarket.com is one place to start; however, using a reputable company is your best bet

Maps

It might be that Google Maps can do it all for you, but I've got some other suggestions just so you have the choice.

- The AA Route Planner helps you to find out how long it takes to get from one place to another, be that your school run or commute, or to pass on to family and friends who are visiting, https://www.theaa.com
- www.commutefrom.co.uk is a handy site that calculates commute times into London, and if that's you, https://tfl.gov.uk is a no-brainer to have on your phone.
- If you want to get to grips with a new city, pretty much anywhere, Citymapper is a good place to start, www.citymapper.com
- Need to find a route, ViaMichelin is a nifty app for you to try, https://www.viamichelin.co.uk

Property Sites and Accommodation

From full moving sites to comparing locations and tracking crime, these are all handy sites that you might want to bookmark for your relocation adventure.

- Airbnb is an option for both site visits and short-term lets when you arrive, so don't count them out, www.airbnb.co.uk

- Compare My Move does what is says on the tin: it compares conveyancers, chartered surveyors and removal companies, so you can save time, money and stress when it comes to your move, www.comparemymove.com
- Rightmove. As well as having all the property to buy and rent, they have a great removal company finder too, www.rightmove.co.uk
- Gumtree can be helpful for finding rooms to rent, temp jobs and second-hand furniture so don't discount it, www.gumtree.com
- Nethouseprices gives details on how much a property was sold for in the past and can be helpful when making an offer on a new home, www.nethouseprices.com
- Want to know more about a location, head to the Property Detective, www.propertydetective.com
- Spareroom is great if you need a temporary base, www.spareroom.co.uk
- Stacks is an online property service that is easy to use and full of great advice and help, https://www.stacks.co.uk
- Need a quick sale? WeBuyAnyHome could be worth a gander, www.webuyanyhome.co.uk
- For reliable information on where to move to, the consumer website Which? has advice as well as a cool comparison tool to compare your favourite places, https://www.which.co.uk
- Zoopla is another property portal, www.zoopla.co.uk.

Personal Support

Yes, there's the practical stuff when relocating, but successfully starting over means good physical and mental well-being. Some resources to help you get this right are below.

- The Blurt Foundation have some excellent resources if you're feeling anxious and overwhelmed, www.blurtitout.org

- Think a little meditation could help keep things real? Try Calm, www.calm.com. Headspace is another popular option, www.headspace.com
- If you're suffering abuse, Refuge are a good starting point for support, please don't do this alone. Take a look at https://www.refuge.org.uk but remember to clear your browsing history if you're in a controlling, coercive relationship, and if you're trying to leave and are in danger, call 999
- If you're finding it hard to cope – and moving is hard work at times – Rethink has some helpful advice and information, www.rethink.org
- Samaritans are there to talk if it gets too much, and are on hand 24/7 via https://www.samaritans.org
- Think some yoga could help you to chill out but can't get to a class? Yoga with Adriene has some great online classes, free and paid, so you can do your downward dog and child's pose from anywhere in the world, at any time of the day, www.yogawithadriene.com

Selling Sites

You can't take it all with you, so as well as giving stuff to family and friends and donating to charity, you can sell items and make space and cash! eBay, Vinted, Vestiaire Collective, Zapper, SimplySell, Facebook Marketplace and Music Magpie are just some of the sites on offer.

Travelling

From day trips to holidays and then the final move, you could be clocking up quite a few miles when you move, so I've got some resources to help with that, too.

- Got to catch the train? The Trainline has an app and website so check them out, it's so much easier than battling trackside queues, www.thetrainline.com

- National Express offers coaches from Land's End to John O'Groats, and while travel times are longer than taking the train, it's cheaper, so worth thinking about. From memory, there's a lot of luggage space, maybe not for a whole house, and they have a buffet service and loos on board, https://www.nationalexpress.com/en, oh and they do airport stops, too
- Skyscanner is great for getting flights at a good price, www.skyscanner.net

Acknowledgements

They say it takes a village to raise a child, but when it came to writing this book, an entire global community rallied around and helped me to get this beauty out into the world.

I've been a relocation junkie my entire adult life. At eighteen I moved from town to city, then from one continent to another, and back again. I went from one London postcode to another, from city to town, town to village, and village to coast. Each move created the rich tapestry of my life, and people from each part of my journey have helped make this book a reality. Thank you.

However, it's my husband and two sons who are the driving force behind my books, and this one is no different. When your wife says she wants to up sticks and go and live by the sea, it takes a pretty brilliant man to put his business, family ties and friendships on the line to make her happy.

By Oliver embracing such a brave move, we saved our marriage and glued our fragmented family back together. Relocating gave us not only the inner sanctum we'd been craving, but also a sense of peace and calm after six years of brutal surgery for our youngest son and ongoing upheaval for his brother. Thank you, Oliver, Eddie and Lucas, for believing in me, and always checking I had a supply of coffee, cake and Diet Coke at my desk as I wrote.

Thank you to all of the experts who contributed to this book to ensure that you, the reader, have the most comprehensive guide to relocating. There isn't a one-size-fits-all approach to relocation and I hope that my words, and the wisdom of the experts who contributed to this book, as well as the comments from those people who have made a big move, have shown that there is more to moving than checking lists and packing boxes.

With that said, I'd like to thank all the experts who gave up their time to help me, and you, and these include: Suzanne Betlem, Personal Trainer; Ellie Cavale, Vets on the Common, London; Judy Claughton, Happiness Ambassador, Meditation Teacher and Well-being Trainer through BalanceTime.co.uk; Jacqui Doyle, Yoga Teacher, www.yogabyjacqui.co.uk; Tony Gibson, Founder of Clearooms; Olivia Heyworth, Creative Director and Owner of Heyworth Gordon; Simon Lockyer, Headmaster at Royal Hospital School; Katie Griffin, Owner and Director, Sawdye & Harris, https://www.sawdyeandharris.co.uk; Poppy Jakes, Poppy Jakes Photography, www.poppyjakes.co.uk; Phil Leivesley, Senior Mortgage Adviser at award-winning mortgage broker MB Associates, www.mbassociates.net; Charlie Lemmer, The Healthy Home Therapist, www.thehealthyhometherapist.com; Michael Padraig Acton, a psychological therapist, counsellor, and systemic life coach; Ben Small, CeMAP, mortgage and protection adviser; Pamela Spence, Medical Herbalist, www.pamelaspence.co.uk; Anna Thomson, Reg. Nutritionist BSc Nutr. Med. mBANT CNHC, www.kandonutrition.com/www.nourishingfamilies.co.uk; Laura Toop, grief and life coach, www.thelossconnection.co.uk; Oliver Trice, Surveyor at Wilde Trice, www.wildetrice.co.uk.

I know that even when it's a move you've dreamt of for ever, the process can be confusing, anxiety-inducing and downright exhausting, so I hope my words help not only with the practical elements of packing boxes and getting to grips with somewhere new, but with the emotions that come into the moving mix, too.

Family, friends, social media buddies and work colleagues, thank you for answering my endless questions and cheering on my word count.

Thank you to Tom for commissioning this book and for his support to ensure that *How to Relocate* had the right words, the right cover, the right spine and to ensure my book got out there to help you.

Thank you to Kelly, Donna, Lucy and Holly for being my biggest cheerleaders, for keeping me going with voice notes and messages to ensure I stayed on the path to book-three completion.

And thank you for reading this book. I hope it has helped inspire and inform you on how to relocate and successfully start over somewhere new.

From the beginning I've said it's not always going to be plain sailing and you could be challenged in ways you didn't think were possible. Your doubts might be real, they could be fuelled by those who simply want things to carry on as they are, but the reality is life is short, and you deserve to be happy. You might not be able to make your move now, you might have made it and hate it, or you could be living the dream.

Whoever you are, wherever you're reading this and whatever is happening for you right now, be kind to yourself, follow your heart, but make sure you also listen to your head and your bank manager, and find a place to call home that allows you to be absolutely, totally, 100 per cent you.

Life's a journey, a series of adventures that enrich you as a person, and it's only when we experience new places, new people and new cultures that we can truly find ourselves and find our real home.

Home is more than bricks and mortar, it's more than the cars in the drive, and so much more than the size of your back garden and the number of bathrooms you have.

Home is where your heart is, where your soul resides, and when you find that place, you can successfully start over somewhere new.

I wish you love and luck in your travels and relocation and if you liked *How to Relocate*, drop me a line and let me know. Please leave me a review online so more people can find out how they can make a move that on their own feels scary.

Natalie

Index